piano PROFESSIONA

The Psychology of Piano Technique

Murray McLachlan

Produced and distributed by

FABER *ff* MUSIC
PUBLISHING SERVICES

*To past, present and future friends, colleagues and students
at Chethams School of Music.*

All rights administered worldwide by Faber Music Ltd
This edition first published in 2017
Bloomsbury House 74–77 Great Russell Street London WC1B 3DA
Music setting by MusicSet2000
Cover and text designed by Susan Clarke
Printed in England by Caligraving Ltd

ISBN10: 0-571-54031-7
EAN13: 978-0-571-54031-0

Contents

Acknowledgements

This book would not have been written without the support and encouragement of the management committee of EPTA UK, to whom I am extremely grateful. Many of the chapters originated in articles written over the years for *International Piano*, and several also originally appeared in *Pianist Magazine*. Huge thanks are therefore given to editors of both magazines over an extended period, and these have included Julian Haylock, Chloe Cutts, Claire Jackson and Owen Mortimer (*International Piano*), as well as Erica Worth (*Pianist Magazine*). Additionally, I would like to thank Lesley Rutherford for project managing this book and to Rebecca Castell for editing. Special thanks to Matthew McLachlan for creating the music examples, as well as to Mark Goddard and David Candy at Spartan Press.

In a broader sense, I remain extremely grateful to all the students and colleagues I converse with on a daily basis at Chetham's School of Music, the Royal Northern College of Music and in countless other contexts at home and abroad. Sharing and exchanging ideas remains an essential way for thoughts and concepts to crystallise with conviction, and I am especially grateful to my main piano teachers Norma Fisher, Ronald Stevenson, Peter Katin, David Hartigan and Ryszard Bakst for so much. Ronald Stevenson's chromatic contrary scale fingering and the excerpt from No. 3 of his 'Contrapuntal Studies on Chopin's Waltzes' is reproduced with the kind permission of The Ronald Stevenson Society and the composer's widow, Marjorie. In terms of this particular book I wish to acknowledge invaluable conversations with Dina Parakhina as well as with Douglas Finch, Philip Fowke, and Madam Zhu Yafen. I always benefit greatly from conversations and musical experiences with my piano students, but for this book, and particular topics that it touches on, special thanks are given to Julian Clef, James Ellis and Arsha Kaviani. I also want to pay tribute to my long-suffering family and to the many informal and apparently light-hearted verbal exchanges I have had with Callum, Rose and Matthew which have all had important impacts on the way in which this book has developed. Above all else I am indebted to the long and extended discussions and exchanges which have taken place with my wife Kathryn Page. It is unquestionably an extraordinary privilege and joy to live with such a wonderful pianist. Her patience, tolerance, encouragement and positivity, whilst dealing with my writing over many years, continues to be a source of personal amazement.

Preface

Happiness, success and confidence in piano playing starts and finishes within the mind-set of the pianist. Thoughts, feelings and visualisation are everything; if you feel worried that you may hit wrong notes at the beginning of *La Campanella* immediately before you start to play it, then you will assuredly hit wrong notes throughout your performance. If you worry about forgetting your Bach fugue in the green room before you go out on stage to perform it, then you will most certainly forget it. Conversely if you have a real sense of confidence and success before starting to play whatever repertoire you are about to share with your audience, then positivity and conviction in your performance is assured.

The Psychology of Piano Technique is the fourth book in the ongoing 'Piano Professional' series – an exciting collaboration between Faber Music and EPTA UK. It is hoped that EPTA's values of supporting and encouraging piano teachers and their students will be given continued stimulus and inspiration from this gradually evolving series of books relating to the piano and teaching. *The Foundations of Technique*, the first of these books, came to the conclusion that 'technique is about putting into practice everything that you wish to fulfil'. This principle is extended and explored in a wider musical context in the second book, *Piano Technique in Practice*, whilst the third book, *The Mindful Pianist* deals specifically with focus and engagement. Its concluding sentence stands as a Prelude to the current volume: 'If we set ourselves up to fail, we certainly will, but if we plan to succeed, and make it possible to achieve something rather marvellous, we just might.'

In fact, *The Psychology of Piano Technique* goes further than 'just might' in its belief that 'success' is unquestionably assured, provided we emotionally convince ourselves that it will happen and needs to happen. It begins with a call for self-love as the vital 'technique' for musical development, and argues that happiness, comfort and inner contentment are seen as essential 'technical tools' for piano mastery. Clearly, alongside physical preparatory exercises, pianists also need mental warm-ups in order to set the scene for a healthy and fulfilling daily musical routine. Avoiding the word 'work' is seen as important in a creative context. We should never forget that we 'play' rather than 'work' the piano! Certainly, we should do all we can to airbrush away any sense of labour or drudgery in the teaching or practice room; in both lessons and practice time, flow and 'playfulness' should always be seen as top priorities.

Though this book deals with enormous subjects including stage-fright, inspiration, injury, long-term development strategies, short-term tactics for success, and authenticity, the over-riding message is a simple one: approach all of the challenges of piano playing from a positive cast of mind – a comfortable, joyful and calmly creative way of thinking. The world may be a competitive marketplace, but your own music making is not. Cherish and cultivate inner strength and enthusiasm. Love your piano playing and music making and they will love you! By focusing on the music and ignoring negativity, your playing will never stop growing.

Murray McLachlan, 2017

Part 1
All you need is love!

Self-love and positivity

Before dealing with pianos we need to deal with ourselves. Love yourself! Take time to nurture and appreciate every moment of your life, every aspect of your day-to-day existence from the smallest and most trivial of actions through to the most glamorous aspects. Be mindful![1] Feel gratitude for everything that you experience. Breathe, smile, think positively and live healthily!

Strong self-love is the answer to so many problems and issues that musicians may have. Through the course of this book we will see that ultimately love is the answer to everything in piano playing. This cannot be stressed strongly enough. Without self-care, nurture and confidence-building, it is hard to fulfil your potential as a pianist. We will see that a lack of motivation, structure and discipline stems directly from a lack of love. Its absence or misdirection also accounts for the root causes of stage-fright, anxiety, artistic stagnation and poor motivation, as well as technical and health issues. All you need is love! It is the most positive, powerful and healthy phenomenon in the universe. Consequently, it is what piano playing thrives upon.

In order to fulfil your true potential as a musician, in order to grow healthily and creatively throughout your playing career, it is essential to adopt as positive and loving an approach to music making and indeed to life as possible. Thoughts and feelings that lack love have no place in a serious pianist's development. Negativity in all of its manifestations – direct and subtle – serves no healthy purpose and consequently needs to be avoided at all costs.

For many musicians, following a strictly positive regime in their lives can prove challenging. Our art requires the highest of standards and, in the pursuit of perfection, many of us have experienced years of tuition from teachers who, through the best of intentions, often tend to highlight problems and shortcomings as a priority, before mentioning any positive attributes. It is certainly all too easy for pianists to be too hard on themselves, to indulge in self-punishment and criticism over even the smallest of blemishes. In the CD era of note-perfect 'white' pianism, pianists can over-obsess about accuracy.[2] Pessimism and forebodings of failures to come will inevitably lead to a lack of success. If these are indulged in the run up to a concert, then a picture of failure will be imprinted beforehand in the pianist's mind that is hard to shift during the concert itself.[3] Inevitably this will lead to a poor or underwhelming performance.

Of course, negativity does not just affect concerts – it can ruin practice, cause disillusionment and turn a bright and optimistic budding young musician

---

1 A good start in this process would be to read Mark Tanner's *The Mindful Pianist* (Faber Music, 2016).
2 See page 130 of Murray McLachlan, *Piano Technique in Practice* (Faber Music, 2015) for more detail on 'white' pianism.
3 In short 'you become what you meditate on'. (Colin Decio in *The Mindful Pianist*, 18)

into a teenager who no longer wishes even to listen to piano music, let alone practise it.[4] In short, negativity is as powerful a visualisation tool as positivity, which means that we need to work extremely hard on a daily basis at visualising, feeling and believing in successful musical outcomes for our playing.[5] Because of this, it is vital to begin, or 'pre-begin', piano playing each day with mental warm-ups rather than a dose of Hanon, Beringer, scales and Czerny. Physical warm-ups and studies at the piano are essential, but they will not maximise their potential to help you if you lack self-esteem, are feeling negative, angry, lack-lustre or less than sparklingly positive. Let Hanon and Czerny wait until you have warmed up your heart! Begin your day with affirmations of positivity; mental lists of gratitude for what you have enjoyed and experienced the previous day. Look forward to things to come with child-like wonder and hope. In short, make sure that you have sufficient loving energy and enthusiasm each day before you start exploring at the keyboard!

In 2016 I was privileged to meet the exceptional Chinese piano teacher, Professor Zhu Yafen, in Shenzhen at the 'Lang Lang Music World' school. Professor Zhu taught Lang Lang from the age of four for six years, having an extraordinary influence on the world-famous pianist. I asked her what Lang Lang was like as a young child, and she had no hesitation whatsoever in confirming that he was full of happiness! His single-minded devotion to music, his confidence and extraordinary enthusiasm for the piano went hand in hand with his charismatic personality. Even as a young child he was literally overflowing with positivity and love.

In order to make the most of our playing we need to make the most of our lives. This means doing everything possible to cultivate good mental health.[6] We can then nurture our love not only of piano playing, but of life itself. An unhappy pianist is more likely to produce unhappy performances; if you are not positive when you play, how can you expect your listeners to be positive? In the pursuit of happiness, we would do well to remember words popularly attributed to Charlie Chaplin: 'A day without laughter is a day wasted'. We do not 'work' at the piano – we play it, and playfulness goes hand in hand with love.[7]

---

4 Of course, there are many other scenarios, too numerous to mention here, such as the way negative thoughts can build towards cynicism in teachers, nerves in adult amateur players, or tendencies in conservatoire students to be critical about everyone else's playing but their own.

5 'Every day we need to fall in love with the piano all over again, and this act of being generous with ourselves … is the route out of the maze.' (*The Mindful Pianist*, 19)

6 This is not a 'self-help' book! The market is currently saturated with a vast literature of 'popular psychology' books which deal with mindfulness, positivity, living 'in the moment' and so on. Examples of this genre, which may well prove stimulating and helpful, include books written from a religious standpoint, such as those by Norman Vincent Peale, through to more recent ones by Susan Jeffers (*Feel the Fear and Do It Anyway*, Century, 1987), and Rhonda Byrne, who has achieved astonishing popularity with *The Secret* (Simon & Schuster, 2006) and its sequel publications. Popular psychology is indeed a vast and thriving industry.

7 See Chapters 4 and 9.

1 Warming up

In the 21st century, the physical nature of preparing to play a musical instrument is often sensitively and intelligently considered by institutions and individual teachers, but what is often still sadly overlooked is the need to adjust psychologically before practising.[8] Before each practice session it is essential to remember that your brain also needs to 'warm up'. You need to stabilise your mind-set, feel gratitude for being alive, breathe deeply and live in the present. Unless you can first adjust to the level of concentration necessary to make progress, there is very little point in attempting to practise at all! Because piano teaching inevitably involves a lot of criticism and focus on what is going wrong, pianists tend to concentrate on the negative and begin work by focusing on what is least successful in their current repertoire. Sadly, this tends to be counter-productive. It is human nature to build on what is set up and established at the start of an endeavour or activity; if you start off your musical day with an uncomfortable, inaccurate, frustrating or puzzling passage, then the chances are you will continue to feel uncomfortable, frustrated, puzzled and play with inaccuracy. Far better to begin by playing a section of a piece or an exercise which you enjoy playing. This will instil confidence and give you the necessary energy and motivation to continue practising positively and with ever-increasing success. But before any of that starts, you need to think through and meditate on the positive aspects of your musicianship and playing. What follows are some of the ways in which all pianists, even those who are at an elementary level, can mentally warm up at the start of the day, in advance of the first practice session.

Mental warm-ups

1 Sing internally; sing literally; sing pianistically!

We all know the benefits of vocal expression. No matter how unrefined your singing technique, being able to shape, breathe and colour the melodic patterns you are about to practise on the piano through singing will unquestionably do wonders for your awareness of and connection to music. In doing so, you will strengthen your inner conceptions of the music and nourish your imagination. Follow this by singing out loud with love and unadulterated enthusiasm. Go for it! Singing is arguably the most personal form of music making you can

---

8 See Murray McLachlan, *The Foundations of Technique* (Faber Music, 2014), Chapter 1. The widespread popularity of the Alexander Technique, Yoga and Feldenkrais has had a positive impact on the wellbeing of musicians the world over. Having a systematic warm-up routine that embraces gentle stretching exercises and ensures that your hands are not cold before you begin to play is an obvious asset and makes a lot of sense. This should be done both at the instrument and away from it. Of course, music teachers have been encouraged in this direction by advancements in sports medicine. We all know the need to start off with slow work, gradually building up towards the more exacting technical challenges that may face us in our repertoire and studies.

undertake. By prefacing piano practice with it each day you are connecting with your true inner musical nature. You can then continue to 'sing' through your fingers as you start five-finger exercises, scales, arpeggios and pieces. (As an aside, I personally see nothing wrong in occasionally singing out loud as you practise, though that is another consideration!)

2 *Connect to the pulse*

Feel the inner rhythm of your music. You can immediately sharpen up your mental attitude with energised internalised clapping, dancing or bouncing in time to selected passages from the repertoire you are about to play. It is fun to do! There is nothing wrong with physical expression – be it movements round the piano, or conducting your pieces.[9] There is a danger that rhythmic considerations are sidelined because pianists have so many pitches to play simultaneously or in close proximity to each other. This is a great shame as, in most cases, it is rhythmic focus, vitality, characterisation and discipline that determines whether or not performers remain focused as they play. Occasionally it is worthwhile clapping through an entire piece from beginning to end. Pre-playing all of your repertoire as a proverbial clapping, singing dancer will most certainly blow way any negative sluggishness, focusing your brain with energised clarity on the music.

You can also try playing whilst singing the melodic line and bouncing with the pulse at the same time. If you want to sway from side to side and feel as though you are internally as well as literally 'dancing' and playing, then bravo and keep going!

3 *Internalise your music*

All successful sportsmen know how important it is to visualise success strongly beforehand.[10] Similarly, musicians should realise the power of their thoughts. Preview everything internally in your mind before attempting anything at the piano, including fragments from your current repertoire. Internalisation need not be restricted to your inner ear – it can encompass all of the (internalised) senses. Hear, see and feel success before you practise! Take the time to imagine a perfect scenario in an imaginary film in which you are the movie star. Close your eyes and really sense the whole picture of what you are about to do. Imagine smells that you enjoy (in my case it would be freshly ground coffee, newly baked bread, or lavender).

Unless you feel excited, elated and satisfied at the virtual world of success that you have just mentally created, then there is no point in bringing it into reality by playing out loud. We are not talking about vaguely formed senses here – on the contrary: the more detailed and carefully experienced the imagined sounds, sights, smells and feelings are, the more successful your practising (and ultimately performing) will be. The internalisation of music is a vast

---

9   Apparently when John Ogdon went to play Bartók's Second Concerto to Ilona Kabos in the 1960s, the great teacher immediately started to dance round the room in the spirit of the music!
10   We will consider visualisation in more detail in Chapter 6.

subject and we will return to it in later chapters. Here its significance is to stimulate a sense of ownership of your music making and the awareness that artistic decisions and energies come from within.

4 *Vary your imagination*

Music is open to an infinite variety of interpretations. There are so many different approaches and possibilities. Often it is not so much what is done as how it is done that counts. To demonstrate, let us briefly examine some well-known Bach. There is something especially invigorating and rejuvenating about beginning the day by thinking, listening and practising Bach's essential works. Here are the opening bars of the C minor Prelude from Book One of the *Well-Tempered Clavier*. Try to 'play' them internally with three contrasted sets of articulation: possibilities include an all *legato* or all *staccato* touch, or permutations of two or three slurred notes with *staccato* notes.

You can extend variety to mood, tempo, dynamics, voicings and colours as well as articulation. The point is that music should never feel predictable. There should always be a sense of youthful discovery; retain fresh innocence and enthusiasm in your preparation for practising each day through change. This can then be expanded upon throughout your 'proper' practice time. Energised mental vitality leads to energised physical pianism; as we think so do we play. It makes sense, therefore, to ensure that our internal preparation for practice is always focused. We can then plunge into as many four-octave precision scales as our hearts desire!

Celebrating physicality!

As you prepare to practise, try and feel a sense of gratitude not only for your music, but also for your piano, the room you are about to practise in, and indeed your whole surroundings. Even the most superficial study of feng shui could prove helpful in making sure that you arrange equipment and proportions in your practice room in an agreeable manner. However the room is set out, however in tune or out of tune your piano is, take time to celebrate and feel grateful for what you have.

Take a few moments to appreciate your own physical armoury, your *modus operandi* that enables you to make music. This is not narcissistic but rather a daily reminder not to take your body for granted. Reflecting with respect on the anatomical qualities that you are capable of is sensible, especially if it is done as you warm up each part of your body in turn. Too often young pianists complain about the size of their hands, their lack of coordination as well as aches and pains and general sluggishness. Physical pain should never be ignored as it is a warning that you are doing something very wrong at the piano or elsewhere. A loving daily inventory of your physique, starting off with some deep breathing exercises, may prevent ailments from setting in in the first place. By enjoying and expressing gratitude for each part of your anatomy in turn as you briefly but calmly move your toes, feet, legs and so on, you are setting up an impressive personal awareness. This should encourage good posture and a calm, sensible, stiffness-free aesthetic for practising. Take care to warm your fingers before starting to play. Flex your wrists gently. Move your neck slowly round in circles in a clockwise then an anticlockwise direction. Lift your shoulder gently up and down. Routines like this are well-known to physical education teachers in schools across the globe, and should be standard practice not only for sportsmen and musicians, but for any individual who uses repetitive motions for many hours each day (e.g. office workers, hairdressers, factory workers etc.).

2 Hedonistic practising

> 'Fill your belly. Day and night make merry. Let days be full of joy. Dance and make music day and night … These things alone are the concern of men.'[11]

Love needs to flow through all of our musical lives. Love gives us energy, courage, concentration and facility. It makes us more creative, sensitive, curious, and focused. Things unquestionably go wrong in our piano playing when we forget about it. Without the buzz of excitement and the sense of wonder, joy and inspiration that come from making music with love, there is very little point in practising. Very few musicians would disagree with that. But how many continuously and regularly focus on a love of music and pianism without interruption? There can be few players who have never experienced at least a little frustration, tiredness, tension and lack of focus at some stage in their practising careers over the years.

Tai Chi

Whilst not an expert in Tai Chi by any stretch of the imagination, I have been surprised to find how many of the simplest exercises from this extraordinary system relate to my own work at the piano.[12] Of course, Tai Chi is excellent for overcoming stress in many manifestations. It can most certainly help with tiredness, tension, focus and frustrations! Indeed, the very first lesson it gives is in relaxation.

Tai Chi's flowing movements and sustained rotations can be used as daily technical warm-up routines to help loosen all of the critical areas used in piano technique. Every Tai Chi exercise begins and ends with stillness, which is essential for visualisation and for energising practising. Both Tai Chi and piano technique are propelled from the mind, and visualisation and serenity are essential starting points for both. Breathing exercises from Tai Chi will help start a fulfilling technical workout at the piano. Try breathing slowly and deeply whilst holding your hands over your abdomen. Feel your stomach fill up with air calmly, then exhale equally calmly. Try this for a few minutes each day, then continue with the same slow breathing as you play five-finger exercises and scales. Next consider your overall posture. The Wu Chi position – a posture

---

11 From the original Old Babylonian version of the *Epic of Gilgamesh*, written soon after the invention of writing and maybe the first recorded advocacy of hedonistic philosophy.
12 See exercises and ideas outlined in *The Foundations of Technique* (Murray McLachlan, Faber Music, 2014).

that emphasises primal energy – is an excellent stance for pianists to cultivate and then adopt at the instrument. Stand with your feet shoulder-width apart, facing forward. Let your hands loosely hang at your sides whilst relaxing your shoulders. Next, slowly bend your knees so that your torso is lowered by about ten centimetres. Keep relaxed and feel light as you hold yourself in this new position for two to three minutes before standing up. Keep your feet firm whilst focusing on a 'lightness' in your wrists, elbows, neck, shoulders, mouth and spine.

After working on visualisation and breathing exercises away from the piano, it is helpful to sit at the instrument and recapture the same feeling of firm feet and fingertips whilst playing. The musical excerpt below (Busoni, *Berceuse*, bars 18–21) works well as a warm up as its hushed sonorities and slow, wide intervallic movements require relaxed arm weight and light, unhurried agility. It encourages a sense of loving awareness of all of your body as you play in slow motion. It seems especially pleasurable when realised with generous pedalling and can be practised hands separately if it appears too challenging at first.

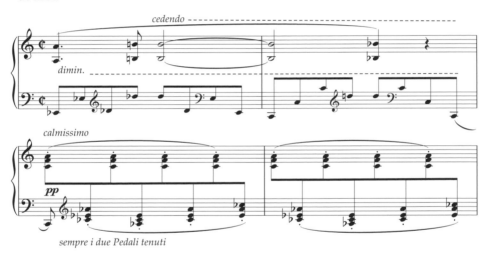

sempre i due Pedali tenuti

We can adopt principles from Tai Chi to focus on the wrists. From the Wu Chi standing position, try raising both arms until they form a 90° angle with your torso. Breathe deeply, prioritising lightness and freedom, and shake both wrists continuously – first up and down, then in rotary movements. Chopin's 'Revolutionary' Étude is an ideal vehicle for exploring this.

Try to replicate the degree of easy mobility from the wrists as you play. Again, it may be best to try each hand separately; continue to breathe slowly and remember to feel as light and free as possible. Only the feet and fingertips should feel firm and 'anchored', to the floor and keyboard respectively.

There are many important elementary Tai Chi exercises that will help relax the neck, shoulders and spine. Needless to say, they can help freedom beyond measure. In the most difficult repertoire, freedom is not sufficient: it needs to be synchronised with economy of movement and concentration of effort. This can be clearly seen in Schumann's *Toccata*:

Progress can be made here if the player grips from the fingertips on each double note whilst simultaneously releasing all stiffness and tension in the wrists, elbows and shoulders. Remember the feeling of anchorage from the feet experienced when standing in the Wu Chi position. In slow practice of the Schumann, the fingertips can be regarded as the equivalent of the feet. Imagine them as the important foundational rocks on which your pathway through this ferociously difficult work can be successfully realised. It is only through loving, persistent and repetitive practice in minute sections at the slowest of tempos that progress can be made here, but that should not discourage students from Herculean effort! When coordination has been successfully realised, challenges relating to stamina and tiredness will cease to exist. The euphoria and exhilaration of conquering the most challenging pianistic mountains makes all of the (loving) effort worthwhile! By concentrating and checking for tension and anxiety in slow motion over the many hours of practice that are necessary for 'success', you are in effect 'scanning' your technique. If you go through this process at the keyboard whilst remaining patient, serene and always physically comfortable, you are using Tai Chi principles to maximum effect and ensuring that you are developing your playing in healthy physical, mental and loving directions.

Comfort and ease: towards hedonism

In the broadest sense, expressive expansion and aristocratic poise is most evident when there is physical comfort. A truly loving approach to piano playing works best when there is an animalistic ease, relaxation and physical joy in creating sounds. Though there is much more to piano playing than mere physical wellbeing, looking after your body is an essential prerequisite for healthy and enjoyable playing and progress. Make sure that you have a sensible pianistic health routine and remain in good shape![13] Diet, sleep patterns, relaxation techniques and posture all need to be constantly reviewed and considered. Do not even think of going near a piano with cold hands! Playing without satisfactory circulation and physical warmth is extremely harmful, as is plunging into fast scales and exercises without gently warming up and preparing your body for practice. Pianists will benefit enormously from finding their own personalised stretching routine before starting to play, and their long-term wellbeing and health requires that a 'cooling down' period at the end of a session is also always in place, so finish your practise sessions with slower, quieter work.[15]

There is a direct parallel with sport, and just as an athlete needs to have good equipment in order to develop safely, so do musicians! Do not use a faulty chair! Make sure that you are not leaning forward to read the notes on the music stand as this can lead to back and neck pain. Make sure too that you are practising in a room with sufficient light. You should feel liberated and at love with your instrument, with lots of space and a sense of wellbeing. There is no harm in lighting a few aromatic candles and placing favourite pictures and objects around your piano if it stimulates a sense of comfort and ease!

With your own personal pleasure in mind as you spend hours and hours at the piano, it is important too that you are mindful of how you breathe, sit, phrase and voice. Tone production and the shaping of phrases will not work if you feel under any pressure or sense a struggle as you play. Of course, stylistic considerations are of paramount importance, but it could be argued that in the pre-advanced stages of learning the piano, comfort and enjoyment from the fingering used should be the number one priority. If small hands need unessential notes replaced, spread, or simply deleted completely, then so be it; far better to 'cheat' a little than to suffer from tension, stiffness or simple ungainliness as an 'impossible' stretch is attempted.

Comfort is an important prerequisite when considering the tempo or the use of *rubato* in any piece. There is no point in attempting to play at a speed which feels 'dangerous' or out of control. Taking a slightly slower tempo than is ideal can lead to a heightened sense of fulfilment, especially if the extra time gained enables more details to be captured and projected convincingly.

Hedonistic practising

Hedonistic practising is all about enjoying what you are doing. It can be stimulated by a deep love of sound, a joy in tonal variety, an appreciation of *cantabile*, and a desire to take tactile pleasure in all that you play. Find ways to maximise the net pleasure of the music you are studying by gloating lovingly over luscious harmonies, extending expansive intervals to the point of self-

13 See Chapter 1 of *The Foundations of Piano Technique*.
14 See www.warmupsandstretchesforpianists.wordpress.com for lots of ideas.

indulgence or decadently over-projecting bass lines and inner voices. If you are truly 'in the zone' while you practise, you will be blissfully carefree with regard to time management. You will want to extend the possibilities of the music you are playing beyond the remit of the composer's intentions. You will search and seek out new and expansive possibilities from the notes on the printed page so that you become familiar with all aspects of the composition to an exceptional extent. 'Hedonistic practising' means that you are truly in love with the feeling of work rather than just with the idea of accomplishing a task successfully.

We can use a multi-textured, vocally-inspired hedonistic approach when practising Chopin's celebrated Nocturnes. In bars 11 and 12 of the famous E flat Nocturne, Op. 9 No.2, the top line is most important and needs nurturing in order to create an appropriately wistful, nostalgic sense of breathing and lyricism (lots of singing and careful listening, with many repetitions in practice, is essential).

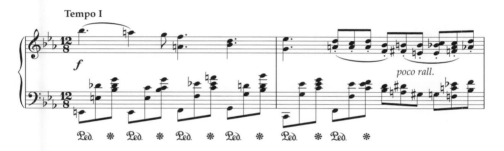

In order to really maximise inspiration and loving familiarity with the lower voices of this passage, it makes sense – in the private confines of your practice room – to extract the leaning notes and their resolutions in the upper left-hand part (the top notes on the second quaver of each beat) and enjoy shaping them as though they were the main melodic interest. Exaggerate the projection of these when practising the whole passage, deliberately hiding the top melody so as to emphasise the beauty of the dissonant D flat as it resolves into C, then focusing on the E flat melting into the D. You can then look further down the texture and highlight the lowest notes for soloistic treatment: bring the fifth finger of the left-hand line into exaggerated shape by making it the main melodic interest. Obviously, this sort of polyphonic practice is extremely useful for making you familiar with the subsidiary voices in a passage, but the main concern when you are working in this way should be to have pleasure and enjoyment in the sounds you are creating. Distorting the perspective of music for the sake of practising makes the instrumentalist feel something of the composer's sense of discovery, and is therefore highly stimulating.

We can go even further in music that is extremely physical, brilliant and mechanically onerous. Working at length on repertoire that needs to fizz and sparkle with percussive brilliance can be extremely tiring and potentially harmful to your health as physical tension can lead to injury. So, try turning 'bravura' passagework into proverbial Nocturnes. The final Variation (No.24) in Rachmaninov's *Rhapsody on a Theme of Paganini* is a case in point. The example below shows the solo part from figure 75.

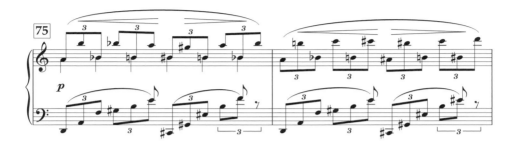

This Variation needs carefree abandon and virtuosic 'dare-devilry', but in order to become truly familiar with the rich polyphony and detail that is prevalent in every bar it is necessary to feel that you have time in practice to sit on each dissonance, wallow on every interval, and celebrate each individual line. Work at these two bars very slowly. Enjoy the right-hand thumb's chromatic semitones alone and then in combination with the fifth finger's chromatic shifts in the upper voice. Both need contrasted colours. Meanwhile in the left hand you can sing, then play, the whole 'accompaniment' as though it were the main melodic interest. Try highlighting the descending minor second motifs in the fifth (D moving to C sharp) and second fingers (A to G sharp) alongside the ascending minor seconds in the thumb. Repetition and exaggeration in practice is highly pleasurable and invaluable when it comes to assimilating and retaining musical patterns at all levels.

Learning to linger: enjoying each moment to the full

We can extend this hedonistic approach by ensuring that we take time to make spaciousness, ease and 'aristocratic poise' priorities in all of our playing. The piano repertoire contains thousands upon thousands of notes. When vast quantities of them coexist in challenging contexts, pianists can be stressed. This results in what Alexander Technique teachers refer to as 'end gaining'. Pianists will focus on how to 'get through' a performance rather than on enjoying each individual moment of it. 'End gaining' leads to a lack of rhythmic control, technique, memory problems, and a feeling of impatience that can lead to boredom. It is the antithesis of creative, loving music making.

We must always remember that music exists in the present, and when we play we should try to love what we are playing. Take time to 'gloat' on an expressive appoggiatura. Lean and project sensitivity by extending an expressive falling interval; voice a dominant seventh chord lovingly, with extra weight and depth of tone on the particular inner note that makes the chord special. By expanding in real time significant features in the music we play, we are sharing with the listener things that we feel.

It is important to remember that it takes time to share things. If we adopt too rigid an interpretation of strict rhythm, then we risk suffocating the music we are interpreting. Within the discipline of a basic pulse, there are all kinds of subtle variations at work. This can readily be seen by starting a metronome at the beginning of a commercial recording of a classical sonata slow movement performed by Brendel, Barenboim or anyone else. Whilst the metronome and recording may start in synchronisation, the two will part company extremely quickly. The point is that music has flexibility, and the greatest performers are able to find ways to linger expressively in performance. They highlight features in the music that they feel at any given time need to be shown. Flexibility can also be adopted in order to facilitate technical ease. Let's look at some examples.

The 64th note scale runs in bars 28–9 of the slow movement in Beethoven's early C minor Sonata, Op.10 No.1, can be terrifying to play, simply because they are exposed and centred around white and black notes (tritones: Ds and A flats).

This passage requires challenging, rapid changes in fingering in order to get the hand into different positions. By highlighting the D–A flat tritones in the scale, it becomes much easier to cope with the technical challenges. Instead of rattling out the passage as though it was nothing more than an expressionless glissando, the notes can become vocal, highly expressive and full of personality. Try sitting a fraction longer on the two Ds that are played before the A flats (i.e. the fifth and 14th notes in the run). This will make you more aware of the two tritone intervals. The extra time gained by listening just that little bit longer and more acutely will be enough to make execution so much less of a problem. By 'celebrating' the inherent angularity in the run, you can turn a pianistic mini-nightmare into a pleasurable experience for both yourself and your listeners.

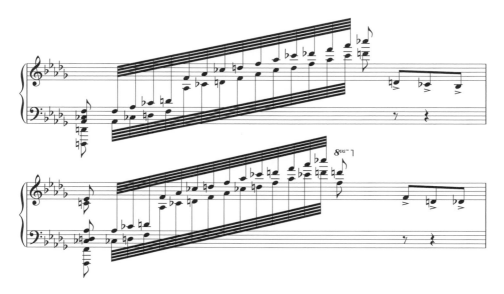

The excerpt above comes from the first movement of Tchaikovsky's First Piano Concerto, Op.23. Though it appears relatively simple (diminished seventh arpeggios presented in double sixths between the hands), in performance the exposed nature of the passage, combined with the fact that the piece is so well-known, often leads to lots of stress. Creative and inspirational help is at hand if you remember that there is the world of difference between pianistic exercises (surely of no interest to Tchaikovsky) and strongly characterised, emotionally charged musical gestures (what this concerto is all about!). First, no matter how upsetting 'mistakes' may be when practising these arpeggios, we should never lose sight of the fact that the melodic line in the passage resides in the single quaver notes. That in itself should make us less stressed if complete accuracy is hard to achieve. However, within the arpeggio flourishes there is ample scope for creativity. If you play the runs in a bland monochrome style with a 'generically cloned' tone, (i.e. no dynamics and a uniform sense of articulation), then you are literally setting the scene for errors to thrive and multiply. However, if you try to add random mini-hairpins (*crescendos* and *diminuendos*) through the arpeggio, balance the hands in a different way so that the left is louder than the right, and 'sit' imperceptivity on selected notes (for example, by adding *tenutos* to the C flats in the left hand) then you should find that your confidence and interest level in practice increase in direct proportion. In passages like these, you need 'good' fingerings from teachers. You also need guidance about how to change position, how to 'prepare' and move the thumbs, and how to work in a variety of rhythms to achieve familiarity and eventual security. Real reliability and inner confidence will only come, however, when you are musically 'on fire'. It makes sense therefore to experiment by lingering on different notes in this arpeggio in turn as you practise repetitively. Pause on the C flats certainly, but then try sitting on the D naturals or even the Fs in the left hand. Exaggerate in practice so that the rhythms become distorted, but try more subtlety in performance so that it is only really you who is aware that you are sitting on selected notes for just a split-second longer than you should!

Another example of lingering comes with the big solo in bars 168–70 in the first movement of Brahms' D minor Piano Concerto, Op.15:

This phrase offers ample opportunities for the soloist to expand, indulge and linger idiomatically, creatively and expressively. The texture should be broken down into its three basic strands and 'worked at' melodically. In the lowest part, this means fully projecting the wonderful wave-like shapes. There is no point in jumping around like a proverbial kangaroo here – this style demands rich sonority and an awareness of string instruments. Turn your left hand into a glorious turbo-charged 'cello with additional low notes! To bow this passage would require *tenutos* on the lowest notes, and so it follows that you can wait in performance on the E flat, D, G sharp, etc. Similarly, you can recreate the bowing of a virtuoso violinist in your imagination when tackling the angular intervallic leaps in the right hand. Its ascending sixths and octaves need to be celebrated. Let the long notes float over the texture. Make the most of the expressive potential of intervals by sitting a fraction longer on the first note of each one than you may be used to. In doing so, most of the technical angst associated with this demanding passage morphs into tactile and expressive pleasure.

When weak is strong

Let's develop the daily 'physique celebration' warm-up from Chapter 1 by learning to overcome a dislike of particular physical movements. Find flexibility and fingerings that give enjoyment. If you consciously avoid using a particular finger, or if a certain type of gesture feels technically awkward, painful or just downright dull, then action needs to be taken! Search for tactile pleasure. Mechanical ease will grow exponentially when you realign every aspect of your pianism to give personal pleasure as you play. The first practical port of call in this inspirational endeavour, from a purely mechanical perspective, is to develop the potential of all your fingers so that you feel truly comfortable when you use them.

Too often fingers four and five are seen by inexperienced players as dangerously unreliable and weak. This is a great shame because each of our ten fingers carries its own strengths, personality and qualities. It is wrong to 'rank' fingers in order of strength. It is equally wrong to try and 'equalise' them. All of your fingers contribute something unique and valuable to your overall technique. The secret is to realise that they all need individual praise and attention. It makes sense to develop each finger as far as possible and from the earliest stages. Unfortunately, conventional scale fingerings make little use of the fifth finger, and perhaps that is why it can remain undeveloped even in relatively advanced players. A lack of mobility and poor articulation in the fourth finger can be put down to the fact that it shares tendons with finger three. We are, therefore, physically built in a way that would seem to discourage this particular finger from gaining its independence!

There are still many teachers who recommend ungainly position changes in fingering in order to avoid using fingers four and five as much as possible. In scale passages where clarity and strength are important, this could perhaps be considered an option. It is also fair enough to adopt this approach in passages marked *fortissimo* or *martellato*. But when we are dealing with *mezzo-piano* or softer levels of dynamics, pianists really do need to find coordination and facility in order to use these outer fingers with confidence and ease.

Exercises

Begin training the fourth and fifth fingers by placing all five right-hand fingers over the five most central white notes on the keyboard (middle C, D, E, F and G). Relax and enjoy the stillness as your fingers rest on each key, then quietly lift up your fourth finger. Keep the other fingers still. If you find this difficult, use your left hand to literally pick up the right-hand finger. Enjoy working your fingers in this way! Keep the other fingers silent and still on the keyboard and try repetitions of F with your fourth finger. Next, do the same for the fifth finger alone; then try playing Fs and Gs with fingers four and five on their own whilst keeping fingers one, two and three silent and motionless. Try to feel looseness in the wrists and encourage a feeling of light freedom as you experiment and exercise. Hold onto your right sleeve with your left hand and literally 'let go' so that your left hand is supporting your entire right side as you continue to play F and G with your fourth and fifth fingers. You should be striving for a hollow, tension-free aesthetic that feels physically good, comfortable and coordinated. Always ensure that none of the other, 'stronger' fingers (one, two and three) move (even slightly!) when their 'weaker' colleagues four and five are working.[15] You should adapt all of these procedures for the left side in 'mirror' format so that you place your five left-hand fingers over the notes below middle C (G = 1, F = 2, E = 3, D = 4 and C = 5). You can practise with fingers four and five in each hand together and gradually develop a gentle rocking, rotary movement between the two fingers so that a trill-like exercise in triplets emerges. Above

---

15 This relates closely to finger independence as discussed in *The Foundations of Technique*, Chapter 3.

all, ensure that you experiment playfully with wrists that remain free and 'unblocked'. It is fair to say that perhaps nothing causes more injury and frustration in piano playing than stiff wrists.

The two examples below show further ways of extending confidence in the use of fingers four and five. The first is taken from the opening of Hanon's *The Virtuoso Pianist*. Begin working slowly and quietly and aim for a sense of ease in playing before gradually increasing velocity and loudness. The second is from Czerny's celebrated *101 Exercises*, Op.261, and should be tackled in a similar way. Both are excellent warm-up routines for intermediate level pianists (players approaching Grades 4–5) and both can be transposed into different keys. As with all exercises and studies, they open up a pathway of development that can be further extended by the student's own exercises and variations based on the original figurations.

Scales

Scales are essential building blocks in most of Western music. They are essentially neutral, but have potential to be positive or negative, depending on the approach of the individual pianist and teacher. Negativity towards scales generally escalates when priorities in practice time favour quantity over quality of achievement. There is nothing more dispiriting than looking at a seemingly endless list of scales on a syllabus and wondering how on earth you will ever find the motivation and time necessary to execute them all fluently and error free. Too often targets for exams make us forget the musical relevance of scales. They become something unpleasant that have to be tolerated so that we can obtain a prestigious piece of paper as documentation of success at a particular grade.

Having said that, most pianists do realise that scales do not exist to make your life harder. When push comes to shove, everyone will admit that they are vital for technical fluency, strength and coordination as well as for the theoretical understanding of most pre-tonal music. Scales are also great starting points for warm-ups, cool-downs and the health awareness aspect of pianism that is so important. Ok, so they need to be fully assimilated, but how can we love the process of harnessing them for our wellbeing? Let's look at four approaches, in order of importance.

1 Tone

Begin warming up with scales, celebrating the beauty of sound production at the piano. There should be a buzz, an excitement, as you strive towards beautiful sounds with each note. Cultivating exquisite tone at the instrument should be a priority from the first lesson (it most certainly was for Joan Last, and remains so for most of the Suzuki teachers I encounter) and should never be overlooked. It is a most inspiring endeavour. Don't begin work with a complete scale pattern as the goal. Begin hands separately with three, four or five notes in succession. Aim for a hollowed, disembodied sound as you play. Touch the notes before you play them so that you start with your finger pads already over the keys. Stroke the keys towards your body as though you are gently caressing a favourite pet. Your tone will become more vocally charged and less percussive as you relax into the keyboard. Imagine that the hammers are tenderly plucking the strings of the notes you are playing, rather than simply attacking them. Slow everything down so that it takes longer to play a note than you could ever have imagined previously. Let the keys appear to gradually sink into the keyboard.

2 The whole picture

It is not enough to acknowledge passively the obvious connections between scales and compositions – you need to mark up on your music all the scale-derived phrases and fragments you can, and practise them alongside appropriate scales or sections of scales. Bringing your musical endeavours into one consistent picture (what Paul Harris brilliantly calls 'simultaneous learning') is a much more effective and interesting way of practising than compartmentalising work on scales, repertoire, sight-reading, aural and background listening. So, isolate a fragment from a piece you are studying. Work on it and back up what you are doing by practising the scale the passage is based on at the same time. Continue by finding something to sight-read that is also based on the same scale. Bring aural into the picture by singing and clapping the passage out loud with the score in front of you, then do it again from memory. Finally, expand your awareness of repertoire by finding similar examples to the scale passage in question and listen to them (teachers should be able to help with this).

3 Tactile and physical pleasure

Feel physically in control and aesthetically elegant as you practise your scales! As humans are built symmetrically, it makes sense to start with contrary-motion scales which not only use the same fingers in each hand for the most part, but also make it easier to feel a sense of stability in posture than parallel-motion scales; our torsos become the proverbial 'trunk' of the tree, grounding the left and right 'branches' which travel in opposite directions before coming together.

When contrary-motion patterns of one octave are mastered, you can move on by expanding the range to two or more octaves, and strive for the same feeling of comfort with parallel-motion scales. Concentration and focus with fingering may be enhanced by silent 'shadow' practising whereby the fingers touch the key surface without allowing the notes actually to speak. Shadow practising is most effective for monitoring economy of movement, change of position and finger independence.

Once confidence and control are in place, we can start to develop speed, strength and endurance as a sporty aesthetic that should be celebrated and savoured. Use the metronome as a proverbial treadmill and build up your velocity and pianistic brawn, always under the supervision of a caring, perceptive mentor.

4 Creativity

Creativity in technique will be considered in more detail later. For the moment, it is worth remembering that scales and scale patterns are neutral musical units which pianists can expand, develop and perceive in an infinitely wide range of ways. The possibilities for perception, exploration and development are limitless. Do not restrict yourself to the middle of the keyboard – try practising scales in every octave range. Don't forget to experiment with different rhythms, varied dynamics, touches, speeds and mixes of all of these between the hands. In terms of colour, even the youngest of students can practise the same scale in different ways: try playing C major over one octave in the left hand as an elephant would (i.e. heavily, with lots of arm movement on each note). Then try it as a little mouse (only using the fingers), as a butterfly (very soft and with less overlapping connections between notes) or as a goldfish (put the pedal down throughout). Of course, with older students we can be more sophisticated and ask for a scale in the style of Brahms, Mozart, Mendelssohn or Debussy (just substitute each animal listed in turn for each composer and the message remains the same!).

3 Playing with flow: in the zone

Practising with the right side of the brain

There has been a tremendous amount written about piano playing and practice in recent years. If you need fresh ideas, pointers on how to work, time management advice or simply reassurance that what you are doing is basically 'alright', then help is most certainly always at hand. Much of this material is highly sensible and practical and presented in a logical, organised way. In short, it can loosely be termed as 'left-brained' advice. As such it should be welcomed, albeit with an awareness that it is feelings, emotions and connections with the instrument and music (right-brained traits) that ultimately lead to happiness and a sense of 'oneness' with the instrument. Left-brained thinking stresses step-by-step progress and analysis, whilst a right-brained approach is more intuitive.

Losing awareness of time, living in the present and becoming excited by the possibilities of musical discoveries and insights are all part and parcel of what can be described as intuitive, hedonistic right-brain practice. It is clearly more positive to take time to lovingly caress the keys and sit on the notes being produced than to feel impatience allied to a need to press on and finish a section of a piece before a certain period of time has elapsed.

Right-brained thinking is all about celebrating and loving the indefinable. When you lose interest in logic and time, it is possible to feel intense energy, excitement and heightened concentration of almost superhuman proportions. It is creative, emotional, curious and random – qualities that lead to 'peak experience', a disregard of the clock, and heightened inspiration. Any experienced musician will tell you that these moments make up the high points of music making. Has there been too much emphasis in piano pedagogy on logic, efficiency and step-by-step methodology? Are commentators in danger of discouraging intuitive and creative approaches by over-stressing the importance of planning work at the keyboard? Left-brained, structured and highly organised piano practice may be politically correct, but it is unquestionably the right-brained approach which will transport you 'out of the box'. You are unlikely to have many 'eureka' moments in your practice if you are constantly checking the time to see how your schedule is unfolding. Let's look at some of the more emotional and intuitive possibilities for practising on a daily basis by taking three famous passages from the repertoire.

The opening of Beethoven's penultimate piano sonata, No. 31 in A flat major, Op.110, could be ruined by over-clinical practising. This is one of the most sublime sonatas in the literature and its first bars need instantly to take the listener into a different dimension, removing the piano from any hint of percussive accentuation. How do you work on this phrase? Having an inner conception of what you need to do is essential. There is no point in playing the opening A flat chord until you hear it – passionately – inside you head. In order to avoid unwanted accents in wrong places, notes that do not 'speak', irregular voicing and a sense of waywardness in the phrasing, it is worth sitting still before you play a note, allowing your body to become one with the instrument. Breathe deeply, allowing your brainwaves time to slow down. Experiment with the speed at which you depress the keys; sink gently to the bed of the keys with each chord. The aim is to feel at ease with the sounds you produce and to allow each chord the opportunity to dovetail and connect into the next. This music requires other-worldly spaciousness and timelessness. These qualities will never be captured with conviction by players who are overly concerned with their watches and what they are doing with each note in the practice room. Let go as you search for your sounds. Allow glorious, spiritual music the opportunity to cast its spell.

In complete contrast, bars 22–24 of Chopin's notoriously angular B flat minor Prelude, Op.28 No.16, present extraordinary challenges in terms of velocity, coordination and dexterity.

It would be all too easy to adopt consistently 'left-brained' practice on a daily basis here as a means towards improving reliability and fluency, though it has to be said that progress can certainly be made from this standpoint. You could work in dotted rhythms or try practising in small segments up to speed with stops (play four semiquavers at a time and stop, then try a minim's worth, then a whole bar etc.). Other logical systems for work include playing the semiquavers *staccato* or 'shadowing' the right hand whilst playing the left hand out loud. You could also use the metronome, and start at a very slow pace (possibly ♩ = 60) before gradually increasing the pace. The left hand jumps could be worked at in isolation and, if any of them are particularly challenging, try transposing the intervallic leaps into different keys.

A 'right-brained' approach to this excerpt could begin in a totally different way. Start by experimenting like an artist mixing colours in a palette. Play a half bar or so of the right hand at different speeds and with different touches and dynamics. What sound are you trying to achieve? Don't worry about how you are making the sound – adjust your approach via your ears. Your body will make the physical changes without your brain being aware of what you are doing. Try to feel comfortable and 'at one' with the keyboard. This is a notoriously difficult number to bring off successfully, so it will inevitably take many hours of work before you can perform it. Patience and progress will be more rapid if you are constantly striving for the sounds you hear in your inner ear, rather than merely working at the piece in a detached manner. It can help to work in a darkened room, or to close your eyes as you play (sometimes tying a scarf over your eyes is more comfortable). If you are really focused on the sounds you are making, then you will not lose patience. You can adopt some of the 'left-brained' methods listed above, turning them into a more intuitive approach, so long as you are constantly listening, and focusing on the sounds you are producing rather than on the 'accuracy', speed or memory. It goes without saying that your performance will become memorised, accurate and fast by default as you work from a right-brained perspective!

Staying with Chopin, the opening of his Ballade in F minor, Op.52, can be cited as a classic plea for right-brained practising.

All teachers know just how frustrating lessons on this notoriously challenging work can be – a piece which can all too easily become riddled with accents, bumps, notes that refuse to speak, phrases that lack natural ease and a general lack of continuity. It is as though students (and teachers) can try too hard. If you attempt to force the music to do what you want it can sound artificial, manufactured and without magical, improvisatory characteristics. In the opening bars you need to let go and literally do nothing! Experience has shown that conviction in performance comes from intense listening in practice, achieved through a sense of calm and relaxation. Open your ears and rely on your intuitive right-brained powers of persuasion … and Chopin will speak!

The flow state – in the zone

Losing awareness of the ego, shedding inhibitions and loving what you do so much that the clock is an irrelevance is a most desirable state to be in when you are practising, teaching and performing the piano.[16] Today this is commonly referred to as the 'flow' state, or being 'in the zone'. These terms were initially created and developed by Mihály Csíkszentmihályi, though they are closely associated with meditative practices that have been around for literally thousands of years via Buddhism and other religions. 'Flow' is characterised by complete absorption in what one does. It implies intense concentration and total avoidance of extraneous distractions. Musicians who experience this highly pleasurable and desirable state whilst practising or performing commonly complain that they cannot remember much about what it was like afterwards. Onlookers note that 'zoned in' performers often appear to find what they are doing extremely effortless, though they are extremely

16   Though clearly if you are teaching in an institution, this could get you into some practical difficulties!

focused. It may be as though they are close to sleep in the sense that they will be totally unaware of extraneous noises, distractions or indeed activities of any kind that may unfold beside them as they play. It is characterised by a state of total relaxation and lack of external physical effort.[17]

Such total absorption commonly leads to a level of achievement that would otherwise simply not be possible, so how can pianists induce it for daily practising as well as for performances? Is it possible to literally 'tune in' to flow?

Csíkszentmihályi may have the answer to this ultimate question: he has postulated that people with curiosity, persistence and who are not self-centred may find it easier to enter the zone than those who are less interested, determined but more self-aware. Positive flow traits have been grouped together to form what is referred to as an 'autotelic personality'.[18] Pianists who can transcend their egos and display at least some of these autotelic qualities stand a greater likelihood of entering the zone than most, so it makes sense to encourage and cultivate these qualities, which are summarised below:

Autotelic personality traits

- Positivity
- A willingness to learn from mistakes
- Interest and curiosity
- Low self-awareness
- Openness to new ideas
- Motivation for the sake of the activity rather than for the reward that lies at its end
- The desire to take on challenging activities for the sake of the activities and the challenges themselves
- Persistence and stubbornness; a refusal to give up or leave a project unfinished

---

17 See De Manzano et al. (2010) 'The psychophysiology of flow during piano playing', *American Psychological Association*, Vol. 10, No. 3: 301–311, which describes a study with pianists who played repertoire several times, eventually getting into the flow state. On entering the zone state the pianist's heart rate and blood pressure decreased and the major facial muscles relaxed. This study further emphasised that flow is a state of effortless attention and, in spite of this, the performance of the pianist improved.

18 'Autotelic' comes from two Greek roots: 'auto' (self) and 'telic' (goal). It certainly implies having a purpose in, rather than outside of, a specific activity. In his book *Finding Flow* (Basic Books, 1997), Csíkszentmihályi defines an autotelic personality as 'an individual who generally does things for their own sake, rather than in order to achieve some later external goal'.

Characteristics of being 'in the zone'

We can develop an autotelic personality by making sure we exercise regularly, eat healthily, keep positive thoughts in our mind constantly, and by incorporating breathing exercises and meditation into our daily routines. Visualising an idealised state of our own, most beautiful pianism should be as important a technical exercise for us to work on as anything Hanon, Beringer or Pischna prescribe. We should also take time to literally to count and remember all our blessings, giving special attention in the moments immediately before we begin practising to all the positive, pleasurable and wonderful things we do and have accomplished as pianists. Looking forward in an innocent way to the music we are about to make is also an extremely healthy and powerful way to induce selfless concentration, which is what being in the zone is all about.

Having said all of that, a word of caution is in order: being in the zone is not necessarily a good thing. We only have to look at the way in which countless individuals have become addicted to computer games to see how its powers, if misdirected, can potentially have devastating consequences. As pianists, we owe it to ourselves not to become distracted by allowing our subconscious powers to be channelled in unhelpful directions. If you really need to improve your melodic minor scales before a grade examination but allow yourself to focus on your favourite Christopher Norton 'Rock Prelude' instead, then you are misdirecting your energies. The 'flow experience', like many other things in this world, is not intrinsically good or evil. It needs careful managing, nurturing and disciplined control. What is certain is that it has the power and potential to make all the activities you choose to participate in richer, more intense and meaningful!

4 Worldly goals, carrots and 'work'

Though worldly concerns are not a priority in the practice room or on the concert stage, we do need to consider the external factors that are inevitably associated with piano progress. How does materialism, pressure from others and the concept of 'work' sit in relation to a love of music? Are there practical conflicts in the 'real world' for the innocent and uninitiated with a passion for piano playing?[19] What about examinations, competitions and prizes? Is capitalism at loggerheads with the values we have been advocating?

If we wish to focus in our music making on an exclusively loving reason for continuing to play, then we need to be emotionally single-minded. A total focus on the music is essential during all practice sessions. We need to be ruthless and reject other 'loves' that can interfere with the technical development of our love of music: fame, fortune, competitive success, worldly rewards and glamour. Let's collectively describe them as 'musical materialism'. They may appear to be naturally connected with healthy musical progress, but if taken to an extreme they are ultimately counterproductive. Of course, they have been used at least to some extent over the years by generations of teachers and parents as motivational 'carrots' to keep young pianists on the straight and narrow road to success. But with the values of the previous chapters firmly in mind, we would do well to take a firm stance against such pedagogical methods. This is simply because they assume that musical fulfilment in itself is not enough of a motivational force.

Fame and fortune: 'But will I make it?'

'There really is nothing like a bit of glamour, a bit of romance, glitz, razzmatazz, mixing with all who are cool, trendy, 'in'. Why else would we buy endless glossy magazines, gaze longingly at our television screens displaying talent show programmes, not to mention the quiz shows, beauty contests, etc., etc. We've all been encouraged to pine and yearn for lifestyles beyond our wildest dreams, to strive to better ourselves in a materialistic way, to be 'right up there' with movie and sports celebs ... Therefore, it is only to be expected that young pianistic whizz-kids long and dream for fame and fortune as they slave away at their instruments for hours every day. More to the point, parents, teachers and agents who associate with young lions of the keyboard often encourage aspirants to expect Liberace-style riches and excesses if they succeed, if they 'make it'.'[20]

---

19 'In the real world' is a platitude of a phrase that is too often used in a way that deflates enthusiasm and inspiration.
20 From a lecture given at Chetham's School of Music Summer School in 2002.

In discussing musical materialism, it is hard to resist satire and irony, if only to retain some sanity in an area where there has been so much exploitation, disillusionment and unhappiness over the years. Of course, it is all too easy to view the world in ruthless, 'dog eats dog' terms. I've lost count of the number of times I've had conversations with parents of talented young pianists which begin along the lines of 'Well if s/he doesn't make it as a concert pianist then s/he can always say that we've all given it our best shot, and s/he could always become a doctor/lawyer/politician/dentist …'. This is perfectly understandable; it is only natural and sensible that caring parents think about the career destinies of their offspring carefully. But at a basic level it totally misses the point – the study of music should not be undertaken primarily because of its commercial potential. Musicians do not 'work' at music. We 'play' and continue to play the piano simply because we love it so much. Career choices come later.

Well before such choices are made, ambitious parents and teachers will find lots of juicily competitive, structured work programmes and ladders for those in their care to climb up. Most of these are highly reputable aids in developing young musicians towards mature artistry. Like many things in life, and in professional development in particular, it is not the tool itself which is 'evil' or dangerous but its misuse. In piano teaching, it can be the overuse or misinterpretation of exams, competitions or concert opportunities which causes harm.

There is nothing gladiatorial about taking the grade one piano examination! If it is entered in a positive, philosophical way, with sufficient preparation, lots of encouragement from teachers, parents and friends, it can be a positive life-changing experience! I joke not: ask virtually anyone who has taken an early grade exam with, say, the ABRSM, and the chances are that they will recall in minute detail the particulars of the ten-minute experience that they had, often, more than forty years earlier!

Piano exams can be extremely beneficial and inspirational tools when handled with care and sensitivity by teachers, parents and the candidates. For a carefully graded scheme of work, using wide repertoire and technical requirements selected by distinguished and experienced musicians and pedagogues, the ABRSM, Trinity and the other leading examination boards in Australia, Ireland and elsewhere offer a stellar roadmap for teachers and their students. If followed through from the earliest stages to conclusion then the ABRSM, to take just one example, offers a journey on the piano from a 'Preparatory Test' (suitable for some pupils after only a few months of lessons) through eight grades and four diplomas. Its examiners and indeed its syllabuses are constantly audited, reviewed and monitored. The actual exams themselves may not train candidates to 'perform' to an audience in a large hall, taking place as they do behind closed doors, and without the requirement to perform repertoire from memory, but the top diploma, the FRSM, does require extremely demanding repertoire, such as one of the last three Beethoven Sonatas.

Competitions

But what of competitions? The 'Festival Movement' provides early experiences in performing to audiences for prizes in Great Britain, Ireland and many English-speaking countries, particularly those associated with the Commonwealth. Competitive music festivals, sometimes referred to as Eisteddfods, number over 300 in the UK. Every one of these is different, with its own character, emphasis and size. There are classes for beginner pianists of all ages, classes for children of pre-school age, as well as those suitable for students at conservatoires and universities. As in the examination world, there is a carefully structured network designed for contestants to make progress towards Parnassus, and the potential for amassing silverware, certificates, even substantial cash prizes, is considerable.

Competitions at all levels are fantastic for the opportunities they give pianists to perform to audiences. If feedback from judges is available, then they are also invaluable educationally. The best adjudicators will offer positive and constructive advice and pianists can learn a tremendous amount from this, regardless of whether they agree with the suggestions!

Festivals, Eisteddfods and junior competitions often lead to larger, more prestigious national and international competitions. Again, there would appear to be a highly structured and intricate web of competitions at the highest level, some more prestigious than others, and individuals are often expected to progress from the smaller competitions to the more famous, such as Leeds, the Tchaikovsky, and so on. But it would be wrong to generalise; often 'winners' seem to emerge from nowhere, to perform with inevitability and authority, and effortlessly slide into a busy schedule of engagements, having been spotted by an impresario with international clout. Perhaps this scenario was true of a generation or two past, for most entrants in the bigger competitions these days are indeed seasoned campaigners who have certainly got used to the unique pressure and stress of competing. There is something reassuring about the neat classification of so many 'brilliant' stars into a pecking order, something that is bound to satisfy the desire of parents and teachers to discover whether or not their young darling has indeed 'made it' or not, no matter how painful and hurtful rejection may be.

Like examinations, competitions become harmful when they are seen as ends in themselves – when they are viewed as a sporting event, when they are used negatively by parents or teachers to pressurise their kids into working, or when they are entered far before they should be. Frequently, many young pianists place enormous amounts of pressure on themselves to 'win' something.

Entering competitions is particularly harmful when insufficient preparation has been done beforehand. A lack of practice goes hand in hand with stress and can be extremely dangerous in all aspects of musical life. Some teachers strongly believe that entry for an exciting event can be a great motivator in itself. Certainly, if competitions can help individuals become more organised, then they can be considered as positive forces. But they should never be viewed as fatalistic, as sure-fire oracles that will decree absolutely what the destiny is of a young artist who may or may not thrive in the unique atmosphere that is the modern day competitive arena.

Ultimately a true musician has no real career choice – s/he is either a musician, or s/he is not. If you try to have a career in music and your heart is not in it, then no number of artificial carrots will lead to artistic fulfilment. And if you passionately love music but opt to choose a career in banking instead, then you also risk an inner lack of satisfaction.

The reason that an artist continues to practise, continues to love music, continues to be inspired not only as a performer but equally as a teacher, a writer on music etc., is because of the phenomenal beauty, energy, creativity and nourishment that the artist receives on a daily basis from music. Go to the proverbial 'creative source' of our art for all the glamour, excitement, thrills and spills and everything else. By doing this you will not be disappointed whenever you fail to win a competition, receive an uncomplimentary notice from a music critic, fail to have a full diary of engagements for the next season, etc., etc. Those who receive inspiration and energy from a deep and sincere love of music will never be poor, never feel bitter that they 'only' teach music to teenagers at the local high school. Mums and Dads need to be educated to realise that there is much more to happiness than a big pay cheque every month for a job that their offspring probably will not enjoy. It is wonderful when one hears of the select few musicians who regularly get the kind of pay cheque all musicians deserve (but most do not receive), but to deprive individuals of their true vocation merely because they could be materially better off pursuing another career path is surely not a desirable option.

Whilst it would probably be misguided to substitute music for religion, the kind of devotion the clergy give to their faith most certainly shows all budding pianists the true attitude to adopt with regard to big bucks, fame and worldly adulation.[21] Material comforts count for so little when compared to the spiritual heights possible through intense study and devotion to the pianistic 'priesthood'.

Ban the four-letter 'w' word!

Work has been seen by many educationalists and parents over the generations as a hard-grinding process, not without its fair measure of suffering, and a necessary chore that has to be endured and persevered with in order to 'succeed'. Under extreme contexts it has been tallied with corporal punishment from teachers, to be practised on pupils who fail to work hard enough! Certainly, the Western world has long held up a work ethic as something of which to be proud. But though it is in many ways based on good intentions, with a strong sense of integrity behind motivation, the work ethic is ultimately counter-productive to a loving musical development.

21 Though apparently the Irish composer-pianist John Field emphatically told a Priest on his death bed that music was his only religion!

'You must submit to supreme suffering in order to discover the completion of joy. Thou, Lord, bruisest me, but I am abundantly satisfied, since it is from Thy hand.'

John Calvin (1509–1564)

Over the centuries, the Puritanical churches have had a decisive influence in this respect. In my native Scotland, Calvinism has historically been associated in the minds of many with an element of self-sacrifice; 'no gain without pain'. In other circles around the globe the concept of 'suffering for success', of sweating in the proverbial fields of educational endeavour in order to 'achieve', is applauded. Indeed, where would the 'American Dream' be without industry and determined sweat and toil on the part of those who have gone from 'rags to riches'? No Hollywood film biopic on the subject of quasi-Cinderella success would be convincing unless the hero/heroine went through a requisite purgatory of work, and no-one is left in any doubt in these ultra-romantic silver screen spectaculars that the toil and strife endured on the road to Parnassus was long, arduous and certainly not at all enjoyable.

It would be wrong to ridicule this concept. It is admirable in many ways, especially if it helps others in our society. The work ethic is great for business, academic subjects, sport, menial labour and countless other things, but totally destructive when applied to piano playing, practice, performing, teaching and encouragement. The four-letter 'w' word is anathema to the magical energy, creativity and stimulus which makes memorising 60-minute masterpieces possible, gives individuals the superhuman stamina to practise up to 14 hours a day on occasion, and gives pianists the dedication and perseverance to do hours and hours of searching at the piano in order to acquire technique, repertoire, confidence and experience.

It isn't just a matter of semantics – it is an absolutely basic distinction. The prospect of 'working' for three hours a day at the keyboard for up to 20 years sounds like a punishment (and it probably does take two decades of practising three hours a day to reach the level of proficiency required in order to be a professional concert pianist).

To sentence ourselves to this and recommend that others follow suit sounds unbelievably 'Calvinistic' in the worst possible sense. But this is what many still believe is the correct attitude for pianists to adopt from the youngest age; those who do not embrace it will remain undisciplined dilettantes without even a basic technique to fall back on.

We have already referred to the platitude of living in the 'real world'. When I perform, practise and teach the piano, I do not want to be a part of the real world, thank you very much! The whole point about our beloved instrument and its phenomenal repertoire is that it transports us way beyond 'work'. We do not need to suffer if we are focused in a musical, loving direction.

Perhaps the piano is not as 'sexy' an instrument as some: the very look of a violin, and the fact that it touches your neck as you play it, immediately makes for a stronger, more basic sensual appeal than a quasi-box with plastic keys, screws, metal strings and hammers. All the more reason for an imaginative bias to be part and parcel of every consideration for the pianist from the very first moment of contact with the instrument as a young child through to the final note in the last recital as an old man. It is always exciting, stimulating and positive to look forward to six or seven hours of searching for sounds at the piano each day in repertoire blessed with the proverbial 'hand of God'. It is always creative in the deepest sense to return again and again to the same repertoire and re-evaluate the same passages in infinitesimal shades, and it is nearly always invigorating and refreshing to practise for long stretches at a time with the realisation that by doing so, there is a connection with a creative force. By returning to the keyboard, one is renewing contact with a spiritual force, getting ever deeper into beauty, truth and strength. Viewed in these terms, three hours a day for twenty years seems too short a time span for piano practice!

With reflection, positive guidance and a continuous love of music, worldly materialism and Calvinistic suffering can be sidestepped and ultimately forgotten. Music can be viewed as a phenomenal energiser, a great quasi-cosmic phenomenon that empowers composers. Pianists can connect on the music-composer-performer 'chain' through the literature of the great masters and so join and share thoughts with audiences, empowering them and indeed themselves in the process. This has absolutely nothing to do with the 'w' word, but everything to do with what life is really all about.

There is truly no reason to play the piano other than because you love playing it! If you love music but do not have a burning desire to share that love with others, fine – continue playing, but don't think of being a concert pianist. But if you are practising with any other prime motivation apart from love, you are in trouble. Find music that touches you, with sonorities that you have a deep-seated desire to produce with your own fingers. What moves you? What piece sends literal or proverbial shivers down your spine when you hear or imagine it? That's the music you should be practising.

5 Love your piano playing and be prepared

'A Scout is never taken by surprise; he knows exactly what to do when anything unexpected happens. A Scout smiles and whistles under all circumstances.'

Robert Baden-Powell (1857–1941)

With our hearts overflowing with love for the music we are playing, for the world and indeed for ourselves, we can sit down at the piano and start to explore sounds to our heart's content. But when we practise an exciting new piece for the first time, our heads tend to send out words of caution. We know that it makes sense to tread carefully – there is no point in going for a generalised overall 'effect' as this will inevitably include imperfections and approximations, and these will be much harder to rectify later. All this seems to be in direct conflict with our emotions. The last thing that we want emotionally is to work at repertoire we adore like a cautious bank manager, plodding carefully from one note to the next. Isn't there a danger of losing all your initial enthusiasm by being too systematic when you practise?

We have all been there: how boring it is to slowly write in fingerings, count precisely and do exactly what the music tells us to do with regard to dynamics, articulation, phrasing and performance directions! It is far more tempting – even if we know it will not do our piano playing any good in the long term – to simply plunge in and drown in a sea of notes.

In defence of left-brain musicianship!

The left brain
- Decisive!
- Logical
- Accurate
- Analytical
- Reasoned
- Practical
- Strategic
- Controlled
- Scientific

Being systematic, ordered, logical and working to a game-plan with a sense of clarity has already been referred to as 'left-brained' in Chapter 3. Dividing your mind in half, with the left side in charge of order and discipline and the right prioritising intuition, creativity and the indefinite may be an anatomical over-simplification, but it serves our purpose well as we learn to cultivate techniques that will enable us to progress and maintain development at the instrument. Finding the discipline implicit in the left-brained approach may be challenging for many; it can take considerable patience to persist in long-term practice exclusively via this approach. If we have memories of a favourite recording or concert performance of a particular work, the temptation to simply play through and try and emulate the musical memory you so admired is always going to be a strong one. And it has to be said that when first looking at a piece there is no harm in playing it through from start to finish – warts and all. This can initiate a sense of adrenalin at the start of preparation that can carry through the focused efforts that must inevitably follow. Indeed, the pursuit of perfection via ruthlessly ordered practising needs to begin as quickly as possible in the preparation process. This is actually true at all levels of playing, from elementary to concert standard. It makes sense to begin hands separately and at a slow tempo, working in small musical units. More advanced students can modify and extend this approach by working at individual 'voices' or parts in the texture, either separately or in pairs. Such an approach is indispensable when it comes to preparing and maintaining interpretations of any fugue or contrapuntal work. Keeping detailed notes that summarise progress on a daily basis will give focus and purpose to this process in an archetypically 'left-brained' style.

Most students do not realise that slow practice is much, much slower for professional pianists than for amateurs. Take the slowest possible pulse imaginable and work at each hand or voice on its own with care. You should do all you can to 'hear' internally the other hand and voices. This will make it much easier eventually to play everything as written together. Even in the later stages of learning it is helpful, even essential, to return to playing your music in segments with one hand at a time. This will act as a 'refresher course' and has the potential to improve both interpretive insights and technical control. We should never take our hard-won security for granted as all pieces most definitely need revision and constant reappraisal. Practising with each hand alone is a simple but extremely effective means of ensuring that security remains in place.

But how do we sustain and maintain our love and enthusiasm for music that we are playing and practising day in day out for weeks, possibly months, at a time? The answer is to stop beginning at the beginning of pieces! Start practising from the places that most excite you, the phrases that you remember and internally recall with the most affection. I once had a very talented student, Arsha Kaviani, who brought along ferociously hard, large-scale compositions to lessons such as the Brahms Second, Busoni and Rachmaninov Third Concertos.[22] Invariably he would begin work in the middle of these pieces rather than at bar one. Naturally, I found this unusual approach puzzling, but when I asked Arsha why he did this, he said it was because he wanted to begin working on the section of the piece that he loved the most. I understood at once – by concentrating immediately on a section of a work that he cared passionately about, he was energising his efforts. We can all learn from this. It is folly to start practising with something that we feel, at best,

22   Arsha Kaviani (b.1990), www.arshakaviani.com

only luke-warm about. Start off in tepid mode and that mode will continue. Begin with excitement, joy and intensity and your work will proceed with even more excitement, joy and intensity! You will feel youthful, creative and in 'peak experience' mode. This means that you will lose awareness of time and feel reluctant to stop practising! Let's continue with some examples of love in practice.

In Bach's masterful fugues we are given so many options, but the primary choice is whether or not we are going to engage from the opening presentation of each subject with or without love. Obviously, the former option is the one we are concerned with here, but if this proves difficult, for whatever reason, then I suggest opting for the power of humour and lateral thinking as a means of positivity. In the B flat subject from book one of the '48', try singing the quaint, eccentric words of the celebrated Victorian composer, teacher and theorist Ebenezer Prout (1835–1909) as you play the notes: 'A little three-part fugue which a gentleman named Bach composed, there's a lot of triple counterpoint about it, and it isn't very difficult to play!'[23]

Saying or singing words to notes is a sure-fire way of engaging a natural awareness of phrasing, but in the case of Bach, this is just the beginning. Provided there is a human element, it is possible to shape and structure melodic contours in dozens of different ways. Use an awareness of breath control, upbows and downbows and imagine colours and the possibilities for creativity through love of exploration.

We have already seen in Chapter 3 that there is so much to love in the opening of Beethoven's penultimate Sonata, No. 31 in A flat, Op.110 (page 29). How sad, therefore, that too many young and inexperienced pianists approach its divine opening phrase with concerns about whether or not all four parts will 'speak', or whether the trill in the fourth bar will be even! I have even seen what appears to be genuine misery and anxiety over how to approach the phrasing here – as though Beethoven was just being awkward to agonise pianists! Obviously voicing, trilling and melodic shaping are important concerns, and they need to be worked at – even sweated over if necessary. But it is wrong to approach spiritual, visionary beauty with negativity. Start with love – in my case that would be singing the first violin part out loud (the music most certainly evokes the characteristics of a string quartet in my inner ear), then continue by deliberately over-voicing the viola part (in the upper left hand). Take time to savour the tenor register of the piano before bringing out each of the other three voices in turn. The trill itself encapsulates and reiterates a deeply expressive appoggiatura, so it makes sense to me to slow that down and extract as much pleasure and beauty

---

23 For more on Ebenezer Prout, see *Piano Technique in Practice*, 75.

as possible. By doing so, by 'searching for the sound' in slow motion, it is possible to lose yourself in the essence of the music's character. It is then a simple matter to return to the first note and play the entire phrase with natural ease and focus.

The opening bars of Chopin's second Etude, Op.10 No. 2, can inspire either a sense of excitement and wonder or a feeling of dread and terror amongst pianists.

Do you look at these bars and see problems of articulation, velocity, accuracy and endurance? Or do you imagine the most fantastic *leggiero* touch, with spider-web semiquavers, shiver-inducing *pianissimo* triads in the right hand and an almost comic characterisation in the quasi-*pizzicato* left-hand part? The choice is yours: you can choose to sigh in melancholic slave-like resignation and proceed by slogging onwards into endless permutations of rhythmic practice with the metronome. You can choose to think as little as possible about tonal quality and feel bored, tired and miserable as a result. Or you can choose to love by always focusing on what is most magical for you. Start as you intend to finish with this latter option.

As you learn to focus with care and affection on every detail in your piano playing, you will find that discipline becomes more and more desirable and attainable. As your love develops and grows, so do your artistic standards, including aural awareness and the objective understanding of your pianism. This will happen on a daily basis, bar by bar, phrase by phrase.

Discipline in musicianship and technique are normally separated when discussing aspects of piano playing. Musical discipline covers huge areas, including fidelity to the text (following exactly all the directions on the music, such as dynamics, articulation markings and rests), water-tight rhythm (including differentiations between dotted rhythms and triplets as well as precision in note lengths generally), awareness of the overall structure of a piece (closely related to rhythm in that a variance in the pulse will immediately upset the structural unity of a movement) and musical punctuation (refraining from accenting resolutions of dissonant notes, 'bumping' on weak beats, and projecting phrasing in a logical and coherent way).

Technical discipline begins with the effective concentration of movements. If a player is finding it difficult to play with the hands exactly in synchronization during a Mozart Concerto, for example, then it could be said that the player lacks the requisite 'discipline' in terms of finger independence and coordination of movements. Technical discipline is concerned with maximizing possibilities with the minimum of physical exhaustion.

In the most convincing performances there is a sense of unity and oneness between the pianist and the piano. Technical and musical discipline fuses into an effortless, organic whole so that phrasing and physical movements seem completely natural, inevitable and authoritative. In great playing there is always a sense of ease and simplicity. In such cases the pianist's hands seem a natural extension of the keyboard. Technical control merges completely with musical intent.

This discipline will only come after many years of loving practice, struggle and thought. But this should not discourage us. As always with piano playing it is most important to enjoy the journey. With this in mind, and from the earliest of stages, it is vital to feel the rhythmic pulse in your body (like a dancer) as you play. With melodic lines it is essential to breathe with the phrasing and sing with the linear undulations. Technically these two attributes will feel easier if fingers are close to the keys and if the general mechanical approach reduces the 'hit' element in articulation in favor of 'touch and press' (i.e. the preparation of notes by getting over them and touching them before actually playing them). It is also helpful to see phrases and sequences of notes together rather than in isolation, and to enhance this feeling of unity within pieces by emphasising linear rather than vertical movements.

Moving towards organic unity

Let's become more specific by examining Liszt's First Piano Concerto in E flat. In the following example the music will only really leap off the page when the figurations are energised and dispatched with water-tight rhythmic control and razor-sharp articulation.

Work towards this by isolating the thumb notes in each hand and building up the tempo from a slow speed until the inner thumb melody line shared between the two hands sounds as though it is being realised by one hand alone. In the excerpt's first two bars the chords need to be practised without the triplets so that they can relate to each other and form an intense, ordered and characterful shape in their own right. As a performer, you need to decide whether you are going to *crescendo* and speed up towards the fifth chord or towards the first chord in the third bar, though of course you always have the right to change your mind. One should never be predictable or repetitive in regard to how you phrase particular passages, and this one needs to have an element of improvisation as well as discipline in order to be convincing.

At first sight this second fragment from the Concerto looks like a transcribed orchestral score. The challenge here is primarily to try and avoid breaks and bumps in the melodic line. It is always difficult to avoid accents after longer notes, and in this case the second note has to be carefully listened to. In a master pianist's hands, it will float out of the first chord. Similarly, it is important not to accent each individual note in the second bar. This whole bar needs to feel like a single, glorious arpeggiated chord. At the same time, each individual note needs to be heard. I am reminded of Edward Dent's description of Busoni's piano playing: '… under his hands the most complicated passages of Beethoven or Liszt seemed transformed into washes of colour, although one could not fail to be aware that every single note was accurately played and nothing was smudged or blurred.'[24] The fourth bar in the same excerpt is much busier. It is written to be played in one long pedal, yet needs pristine clarity of articulation. There should be a sense of one big sweep whilst also caring deeply for every single note; this has to be thought through and worked at avidly if real mastery of the instrument is to be achieved. In this particular case the passage needs to be built up patiently and painstakingly, with emphasis on each individual note, then groups of four to six notes, then in two big sections, and finally in one big sweep. It is up to the pianist to listen carefully and to ensure that there are no 'holes' or bumps as he plays.

The pedaling, as written in the third example from Liszt's Concerto, can lead to heavy accentuation on the low A flat and G in the bass clef of the second bar.

The challenge here is to try and allow the top melodic line to sail effortlessly on through changes of pedal and harmony. This can be achieved more simply if the pedal is quickly raised and depressed a split-second after the A flat and G bass notes in the second bar are played. To simultaneously change pedal as you depress these notes can destroy the passage's sense of line.

24   Edward J. Dent, *Ferruccio Busoni: A Biography* (Eulenburg Books, 1974).

Conclusion

We should not view a left-brained approach to music making as being less inspirational than a right-brained approach. Disciplined, organised and organic piano playing is achieved with lots of thoughtful, considered and systematic practising. Success will come when there is deep concentration, physical comfort and 'peak experience' in the practice studio. Ultimately the highly desirable, left-brained qualities in music making stem just as much from the power of love as the right-brained qualities. We are talking about two sides of the same coin; both thrive on positivity. Systematically airbrushing away negative thoughts from our minds and refusing to say, write or emotionally express anything that is not positive, will do wonders for our piano playing. We should avoid thinking of the passages in a particular piece that we find challenging before starting to practise. Whilst playing we need to think in the present, focusing on each phrase as it unfolds rather than on 'nasties' about to come or passages just played that we consider 'unsuccessful'. And when we have finished playing or practising we need to immediately recall everything that went well, rather than brood destructively on the couple of notes that were inaccurate out of the hundreds that were played securely.

Consciously adopting a 'left-brained' aesthetic for this positive outlook and attitude makes sense. Discipline and organisational strength will reinforce the loving message that is implicit in this approach more strongly than the intuitive right-brained approach. In terms of day-to-day, hour-by-hour left-brained organisation, this can mean beginning each session at the instrument with a fragment of music that we especially like. Find a nugget of notes that make you feel better about your playing, not worse. From this modest but positive starting point you can then continue practising with confidence and enthusiasm, gradually building up an entire programme of repertoire to a truly inspirational level of achievement.

Part 2
Inspiration

Transcending limits

Why do we practise, play, perform and teach? It is a big subject, but primarily we are drawn to our art because it takes us towards something much more beautiful than our everyday concerns. To be infused, indeed exalted, beyond personal boundaries is to be, literally, 'in spirit'. Music is a magic mirror through which our approach to everything is transformed. If you forget to look through it, there is no point to playing an instrument. It could be argued that this is the only appropriate creative starting point for all of our work at the keyboard.

Ultimately inspiration takes us away from our everyday concerns – our insecurities, worries and tiredness. Inspiration gives us transcendental powers to reach way beyond anything we would normally think of as being even remotely possible. Above all, inspiration helps us forget our egos, leaving us free to enjoy our music making at the highest possible level.

6 Creativity in technique

Playing in practice

In Chapter 4 we discovered that the ever-changing energy present in all music reveals itself most when we remember to 'play' rather than merely to 'work' at the piano. Our time at the instrument is at its most inspired and creative when we realise that the many hours we spend practising deserve to be filled with experiments and novel discoveries. View your practice room as a laboratory for playful testing. New dynamics, articulation, distorted rhythmic groups and even transposed passages can take you well beyond the remits of 'straight' practice. You should feel close to the spirit of a composer as you quite literally 'play' rather than 'work' at music. Adjust and extend some of the figurations and sections of a piece you are currently studying in the spirit of creative fun and see where it takes you.

Let's look at the opening of Mozart's famous Sonata in C major, K545, as a starting point.

There are so many different and unpredictable ways in which confidence, familiarity and facility can be developed here. Rather than approaching it literally with conventional techniques (i.e. slow, hands separate work giving mindful attention to the fingering) why not try depressing the keys so slowly that the notes fail to sound at all? Practising in this way forces you to take extra time and care. It also feels like a game – the aim of stopping notes from 'speaking' adds a bit of extra novelty value to what could otherwise become a rather dull procedure.

Continue practising this sonata by tackling each phrase at different dynamic levels. Can you make each dynamic clear and defined? What about varying the articulation? Try one hand completely *staccato* with the other totally *legato*; then reverse the articulation before mixing up touches in every permutation you can devise. Next, think about tone between the hands. Deliberately try to drown out the right hand by over-emphasising the left, then gradually increase intensity in the right hand until you arrive at an ideal tonal balance. Much amusement and rhythmic coordination can be gained if you care to tackle both the opening alberti bass quavers and the semiquaver scale runs (from bar five) in jazzy, 'swung' rhythms. You will also gain much in terms of overall musical awareness if you can sing the left hand out loud whilst playing the right hand, or tap out the left-hand rhythms on the music stand whilst playing the right. Other possibilities include practising with your eyes shut or even crossing hands and playing the bass clef with the right hand and the treble with the left (this latter option normally proves to be especially challenging).

Practice can be extended to potentially limitless dimensions by transposition, helping to sharpen your awareness of intervals and chord progressions and improving musical reflexes and general harmonic 'geography'. Begin with a single bar at first. Try it out in several different keys and see how this changes the character and technical difficulty of the chosen fragment. Transposition can be viewed as the gateway towards composition: indeed, it is easy to use this excerpt as a springboard towards creating a whole library of satellite exercises. Why not play all of the right hand in octaves? Try this in D flat and D major as well as the original key. Try playing the piece using only your second fingers in each hand. Can you do this quickly and lightly (developing dexterity and flexibility) as well as slowly (connecting one sound with another via total relaxation in the wrists and forearms)?

These are just some of the limitless possibilities that could be explored. Use a sense of discovery and openness to retain a consistent freshness and enthusiasm in all of your piano playing.

Creativity

Traditionally, practice tends to be structured into recognisable compartments of time: typically work commences with exercises, moves onto scales and arpeggios, possibly followed by studies, before repertoire is tackled in the largest segment of practice each day. Sight-reading is often left till last. Composition, aural and improvisation training are then either neglected entirely, or else squeezed into whatever time is left at the end of the working week. This seems a great pity, because it is perfectly possible – and often extremely desirable – to fuse and unify aural and creative practice with technical development.

As we have just seen in Mozart's C major Sonata, the simplest way to get started with 'creative' technical work is to transpose exercises or problem passages into different keys. Let's take a left-hand arpeggio figuration from Debussy's *L'Isle Joyeuse* as a case in point.

This apparently simply figure can prove deceptively awkward in practice, requiring good flexibility and coordination. Try transposing this manoeuvre into the eleven other major keys, using the same fingering each time, practising each modulation with equal care and curiosity. There will be subtle changes in the distances between fingers, and certain keys will prove more challenging than the original, but this nurtures a greater overall understanding of the problem itself, and can therefore benefit general technical facility. It can be tremendous fun modulating, and the process of doing so can open up improvisatory offshoots that can easily be expanded and notated as small études.

Transposition not only stimulates and nourishes technical facility – it also provides a firm understanding of intervallic and key relationships and so develops stronger aural and memory skills. Indeed, many memory stumbles result from a lack of security or awareness of basic chord sequences. I strongly recommend that technical difficulties in one hand are practised in the other hand also through modulation, bearing in mind that pianism thrives on symmetrical fingering. Thus, an ascending arpeggio pattern in the right hand is best worked at with the same fingering in a modified descending version for the left hand, rather than as a literal 'copy' that uses different fingering.

The harmonic flavour that results from symmetry usually creates a 20th or 21st century soundscape of intriguing colours. Works as famous as Bartók's *Music for Percussion, Strings and Celeste* and Busoni's *Fantasia Contrappuntistica* lean heavily on techniques of symmetrical inversion, so who knows where your technical extensions could lead you?! Certainly, there is never an excuse for feeling bored with technical challenges.

If you must stick to one-handed technical work from tried and tested authors such as Schmitt, Tankard and Harrison, then do try to play chords and figurations in the hand that is not working. It can be intriguing and inspirational to play five-finger exercises in the right hand whilst adding, for example, whole tone chords in the left. And one should not be limited to monochrome colours in this endeavour – the whole gamut of touch and tone should be considered and utilised in turn.

Systematic technical progress can be made by taking particular problems and 'exercising' them via transcription. Busoni famously used play to melodies from *The Merry Widow* in octaves! In a similar way, we can take popular melodies and work at them in trills, double thirds and sixths, chords and octaves. The motivation to improve becomes so much stronger when a student can claim ownership of the exercise or study he is practising simply because he is the composer!

Perhaps the most stimulating repertoire to use for technical creativity is found in the best-known keyboard works of Bach. Busoni's long out-of-print Schirmer edition of Part One of the *Well-Tempered Clavier* is filled to the brim with ideas and possibilities for exercises based on Bach. The excerpt below shows how Busoni rearranges the opening C major Prelude from the *Well-Tempered Clavier* as a study for the right hand, with none of the actual notes changed.

Ideas from Bach are important in Frank Merrick's wonderful *Practising the Piano*, one of the most creatively charged textbooks on piano technique in the literature.[25] Merrick recommends that each Bach two-part invention be practised with only one finger in each hand. He also suggests that the inventions make excellent octave studies. They can be played in double thirds, sixths, and in different keys, whilst retaining the fingering from the original key. Such practice may prove too challenging at first, but perseverance most certainly leads to superior facility, flexibility and a stronger awareness of the geography of the keyboard. Merrick stresses the importance of singing one voice in a Bach three-part fugue whilst playing the other two (Nadia Boulanger also recommended this challenge) and generally brings energetic brio and sparkle to every aspect of technique that he discusses.

A lot of progress can be made by finding the stumbling block that is preventing a particular passage from working convincingly. By isolating the problem, then working on a whole range of exercises to address it, an encyclopaedic breadth will begin to emerge in one's overview of pianism. It is also tremendously stimulating to 'relate' passages from different repertoire, then practise them all, one after the other. Thus, trill passages in the *Goldberg Variations* can be placed next to similar figurations from late Beethoven, Chopin and Liszt. The most curious students will extend each example, transposing and reworking them for both hands, finding out how to coordinate muscles and fingers in the best way.

Ultimately a creative approach to practising technique saves time – it leads to greater musical understanding and facility, so that more and more challenges become realisable, without having to think about them as challenges in the first place.

Alfred Cortot's *Rational Principles of Piano Technique*

Cortot's celebrated collection of exercises is arguably the most creative available, in the sense described here, of all the standard anthologies of exercises.[26] It comes with a detachable transposition chart which also offers rhythmic variants and which the student is expected to apply to every exercise in the book. Its exhaustive nature and approach can be rather intimidating. But when one tunes in to its uncompromising, encyclopaedic style, it quickly becomes evident that most of Cortot's exercises are simply impossible to execute with any conviction at all without an acute ear, flexibility mixed with coordination, and a consistent desire for non-percussive, resonant sonorities. I am especially fond of many of the exercises on polyphonic technique and the thumb/changing position, for they nurture beauty of sound and advanced finger coordination and precision to an extent not really encountered elsewhere. It is also a wonderful course for emphasising the need for pianists to remain flexible and loose in their wrists, elbows and shoulders.

---

25 Frank Merrick, *Practising the Piano* (Barrie and Jenkins, 1960).
26 Alfred Cortot, *Rational Principles of Pianoforte Technique* (Editions Maurice Sanart, 1928).

Lateral thinking

Many of the frustrations of technical restrictions can be overcome by
approaching problems in completely different ways. This can be seen the
example below – a contrary-motion scale beginning on D. Most teachers would
finger it 1–3–1–2–3–1–3–1–3–1–2–3–1 in each hand, but Ronald Stevenson's
extraordinary approach, making use of symmetry and 'the sixth finger' (i.e.
a slide from 5–5 at the end) will immediately make super-human velocity a
reality:

I would always recommend that students take time to stand back from
technical problems, and refrain from mindlessly repeating awkward corners.
Often a fresh perspective can be achieved simply by adjusting one's thought
processes; focusing on a particular line or voice in a thick texture can take
anxieties away from the difficult jump. It is also worth considering an
association of a particular object or image with the successful realisation of a
hazardous manoeuvre. I once taught a student who thought of an apple when
he navigated through a left-hand passage of ferocious danger, and he swore
that it was this visual anchor that led to consistent success in the passage!

Further creativity via symmetrical inversion and counterpoint

It goes without saying that Chopin's études are of seminal importance, and
many of them are concerned with the development of one hand in particular.
The example below comes from the third of Ronald Stevenson's *Three
contrapuntal studies on Chopin Waltzes*: an exhilarating cocktail which mixes two
of Chopin's celebrated A flat Waltzes into a single whole.

Here, contrapuntal genius and a deep understanding of how the two hands can
work in complementary physical movements leads to a fresh perspective. One
can well imagine the initial gestation of this 'commentary' on Chopin growing
from the Scottish composer-pianist's own practice sessions.

7 Visualisation and inspiration away from the piano

In the sports world, the power and necessity of visualisation is fully understood and has long been standard practice for all kinds of athletes. We have all heard of sports psychologists and the huge benefits that they can have on preparation and development. By picturing success and pre-playing their performance mentally, by working through each step of their sport in miniscule detail, triumphant victories emerge in athletes' minds.

Musicians can learn so much from sports psychology. Quite apart from the hugely positive impact that pre-play mental preparation can have on general confidence, self-esteem and wellbeing, musical visualisation most certainly encourages direct performance success too. Mental practising needs to include both visual and aural pre-played conceptions. A musician's 'vision' should entail an entire performance being pre-played and positively thought through in the inner ear. As soon as we think that we are going to have a memory lapse, strike a wrong note or lose control, disaster will strike. And the reverse is equally true – if we think and feel positively about what we are to play, we will succeed. Therefore, as a matter of the utmost importance, we should ensure that our thoughts are consistently upbeat and positive!

This means that we need to truly believe in our ability to realise our intentions in our piano playing. If technique is about the manifestation of our musical desires, then we need to have total trust in our ability to bring our inner intentions (our thoughts) into the real world. We need a strong, unshakeable sense of conviction and self-belief. In a sense, we need to succeed twice for everything we play – firstly in our thoughts, and secondly in reality!

Internalised films

In sport, positive thinking in advance of action is considered an essential part of training. By repeatedly creating clear, detailed mental pictures of what is desired, sportsmen are able to isolate and focus on each aspect of their techniques. Complete internal confidence and assurance can then be secured.

A good way to begin experimenting with this is to create your own internal movie; a film script entirely within your mind. Imagine a film in which you watch yourself as you would like to be. Self-esteem and inner awareness are given injections of positive energy whenever this film is internally played through. If you can equate the visualisation process to daily meditation, then your positive mental pictures of success will gradually permeate into your sub-conscious, making success and fulfilment in your playing a foregone conclusion. I recommend that you prepare for meditation by lying down on the floor and relaxing; take deep breaths and banish negative thoughts; live in the present. Instead of thinking 'what if I cannot?' simply look forward to playing and experiencing beautiful music. Once you have achieved this, it is time to begin a detailed visualisation of a complete performance.

Let's take a few musical excerpts and see how a mentally pre-played internal film could be applied in each case. The opening of Chopin's second Ballade is mysterious primarily because the music could have been playing long before its first printed note begins.

The obsessively repeated C creates a hypnotic stillness that needs ethereal sonorities free of accents. This is music that floats, ghost-like, off the ground. In visualising this opening it helps to imagine the first bar being repeated many times over. Each note dovetails with the next with a sense of reverberation, glow and quiet intensity; it is as though the piano is humming. Your inner ear needs to have awareness of tonal balancing between the hands, whilst the dotted rhythms need to have both a dance-like grace and hushed expectancy.

César Franck's *Prelude, Chorale and Fugue* turns the piano into an orchestra with organ and harp. In order the recreate the sound of an organ at the beginning of the chorale it is important to overlap fingerwork as much as possible.

In this example, any pre-play practice away from the piano would need to include an awareness of the use of full arm weight. As you internally visualise and hear a perfect rendition of this section, imagine your fingers sinking slowly and deeply into the keys, reverberating and glowing with ecclesiastical intensity and passion.

Later in the same movement, Franck's strikingly memorable and beautiful arpeggiated chords clearly evoke harp-like sonorities:

Harp chords tend to be more reverberant and stately than guitar chords for example, so it is important for the pianist to listen carefully to the afterglow of every note played here. Mental visualisation for this extraordinarily beautiful phrase requires an awareness of touch, pedalling, chordal balancing and phrasing. It can help if you literally imagine you are inside a great cathedral, with a vast spaciousness and reverberant acoustic. Lots of possibilities need to be thought through. Experiment with these at the keyboard and vary the key bedding, length of pedalling and direction of phrasing.

Next, we can examine Debussy's *Clair de lune* in different internalised instrumentations.

Try to pre-play it internally with violins (lots of overlapping *legato*, resonance and firm, curved fingertips for definition of tone). Alternatively, it could be heard inwardly with woodwind instruments at the forefront, (imagine pairs of clarinets and flutes playing the left and right-hand parts respectively, with a lighter touch on the surface of the keys, flatter finger-shapes and less definition of articulation).[27] As in the excerpt above from Chopin's second Ballade, the aim is to produce accent free, floating pianism. But Debussy requires even more of an ethereal sheen in terms of tonal finesse, and this example needs to be balanced with greater intensity in the top-most notes. The silences and pauses on long notes are more magical than the notes themselves, and internal conceptions in advance of literal practising at the keyboard need to maximise an awareness of this.

Practising without a piano

Pianists often obsess about staying at their pianos for hours every day, and indeed students at conservatoires frequently become very distressed when pianos are not available for them to practise on. Obviously, this is

---

27 For a more extensive discussion of how to 'orchestrate' pianism, see *Piano Technique in Practice*, 63–5.

understandable, but I would challenge the notion that a student needs to be at a piano in order to practise effectively and make progress. It could be argued that one of the major causes of insecurity in performances from students comes from their inability to really know their repertoire intimately in their heads. In order to be really secure with music that you are performing you should be able to literally 'play' every note of your concertos, sonatas and pieces in your head from memory, away from the instrument. Once students acquire the ability to do this, their confidence and self-belief tends to soar. They can work away from the piano at each aspect of memory – aural, visual, kinaesthetic (fingering) and theoretical – and by so doing will feel liberated from the physical constraints of having to book a practice room, or feel frustrated by the poor quality of the instrument they own. Simply working on the left hand alone, building up a secure memory of it whilst on a train or waiting for a bus, will make a memorised performance in a big concert hall so much easier. This involves singing passages out loud, looking at the music then closing your eyes and literally 'seeing' the printed score in your head, analysing the music in terms of chords, keys, scales, intervals and so on, then remembering these with the music book closed, and finally literally 'playing' your music on a work surface rather than at a piano! Working in these ways without a piano can be extremely relaxing. Practising in your head can be done when you are lying on a bed, out for a walk in the park, or simply whilst sitting quietly at a desk, making occasional fingering movements on the work surface when you wish to check out a challenging fingering or technical manoeuvre.

But work away from the piano should not be limited to building up memory and technical security. Literally every aspect of piano practice can be done away from the instrument. You only need to think of a conductor's lot to understand this. Conductors need to be alone and 'hear' scores in their heads as they work on phrasing, *rubato*, balance, entries, colour and so on (it is not possible to hire the Berlin Phil. when you are preparing your interpretation in advance of rehearsals of 'Mahler 3'!). There are great advantages to this as it forces conductors to really know their scores.

Pianists have an 'orchestra' at their fingertips in terms of the colours and possibilities that can be conjured out of our beloved instrument. But if there is insufficient preliminary work done away from the instrument, the complexities and physical challenges of piano playing can cause a lack of imagination in terms of interpretation and freshness of approach. Perhaps it is more productive to sit away from the piano and work out internally which specific colours and sounds you wish to project before launching into intensive, repetitive work at the keyboard itself. Certainly, this was the sentiment of the great pianist Walter Gieseking and his mentor Karl Leimer who stressed how important it was to completely memorise a piece of music away from the piano before even attempting to practise it out loud.[28] By doing this regularly, Gieseking was able to mould an inner conception, an idealised interpretation of a new piece that was entirely unspoilt by the technical and practical

---

28 Gieseking and Leimer, *Piano technique: The shortest way to Pianistic Perfection* (Dover, 1972).

considerations that inevitably appear from the earliest stages of note learning. Thus, he began playing new music out loud with real conviction and purpose.

If you find it challenging to hear scores in your head, I recommend that you begin by listening to recordings and follow the score with your fingertips. Listen to short pieces several times at first, then switch off the recording and follow the score again, trying to hear the music. Patience and perseverance are important for success here; if complete movements are impossible for you to cope with, try smaller sections and simpler music from Mozart or Haydn.

The challenges of the celebrated *Funeral March* from Beethoven's Sonata in A flat, Op.26, are predominantly rhythmic.

The relentless, hypnotic repetitions of dotted rhythms in this movement are surprisingly hard to realise with discipline and consistency. Too many performances lose control after even just a few bars, with the rhythms morphing into triplet figurations rather than remaining as dotted quavers and semiquavers. This issue, like so many other rhythmic problems that students frequently encounter, is most effectively tackled away from the piano. Clap or beat out semiquavers on a work surface whilst singing the melody in time from the beginning. You can also try a little physical workout if your practice studio is big enough! Throw inhibition aside and literally march with pronounced footsteps around the room, singing Beethoven in strict time as you go. Each footstep you make should be precisely synchronised with the crotchet pulse. This may be childlike, but it is enjoyable to do, and most certainly effective if worked at consistently.

The opening of the development in the last movement of Beethoven's A major Sonata, Op.101, is particularly treacherous, requiring complete awareness of fingering as well as the ability to consistently apply the same fingering time and time again. In order to focus single-mindedly on fingering, it is very helpful

to 'play' the passage above on a work surface, the piano lid, or even just on
your knees! Working at the piano itself makes you think of too many other
issues, but this 'table top' practice approach manages to keep you exclusively
concerned with the finger patterns.

Let's now return to Franck's *Prelude, Chorale and Fugue* for more inspiration.

This sonorous edifice comes at the climax of Franck's *Fugue* and is extremely
complex contrapuntally. It requires an acute awareness of each melodic line
if security and musical lucidity are to be achieved. Begin by playing each
element in the texture separately on a work surface, singing as much as you
can at the same time. Close your eyes and repeat this process – short term
memory will do wonders for building up awareness, control and technical ease.
Move forward by playing each hand separately (still on a table top!) and then
together, finishing off with as much 'playing' as possible with your eyes closed.
After a few days of working in this manner you can return to your piano and
work with sound. Practising will be so much quicker and easier if initial work
away from the instrument is done!

Further inspiration away from the piano

In piano literature, there are many examples of pieces with descriptive titles
to beguile and lift one's imagination. It is vital to keep these in mind at every
stage in the learning (and relearning) process. Use them as triggers in your
work away from the piano and see where your imagination leads you! Do not
shy away from naivety: on a broad level, we should never dismiss childlike
evocations of pictures as a means of interpretive direction from students of
any age. We can contrast static imagery as one means towards heightened
creativity with kinetic pictures which can lead to another stimulating range of
choices to be considered.

All of this is only natural, and as pianists we can 'work' the visualisation
process in reverse; our music may well encourage the creation of cinematic
scenes in the silver screen of our own private minds. Just as films and plays
have often relied heavily on music for evocation and dramatic tension, so it is
perfectly logical for pianists to reverse this process and find a drama, original
or otherwise, to fit with any composition they are studying. This concept
has been around for centuries, influencing the interpretation of Beethoven's
sonatas from the early 19th century as well as many works by the major

romantic composers.[29] Liszt was famous for writing down words from Goethe and Schiller over passages in various compositions in order to stimulate a pupil's imagination. And in the 20th century Alfred Cortot once tagged on the legend of Ondine to Chopin's third Ballade simply because that was what the music suggested to Cortot's extraordinary imagination.

It can be creatively stimulating to visualise a film screen in front of you as you play over a composition in your head. Try literally re-enacting a complete dramatic plot throughout a whole composition in the theatre of your mind. Whether you choose to feel yourself as an actual protagonist or an observer in the imagined scenario will depend on context. The actual re-enactment of a storyline during a public performance is a different matter entirely, and depends largely on your ability to maintain the requisite sense of distance necessary in order to listen sensitively and acutely as you perform.

As well as imagery, extra-pianistic sonorities, touches, even tastes and smells can play an important and inspiring role in practising away from the instrument.[30] The easiest way to embrace this concept is to set up role-play games. In this first game you are not a pianist – you are a great conductor. The keyboard is the Berlin Philharmonic, and the task you set yourself is literally to make every sound that emanates from your fingers as orchestral as possible. One need look no further than the Beethoven Sonatas to experiment with here, as everything can be considered either from the perspective of a string quartet or a classical orchestra. In working through a section from the 32 sonatas in this manner (for example the slow introduction to Op.81a, 'les adieux') it is most helpful to be as detailed and specific as possible. By so doing there will be much more variety and conviction in realisation, as well as greater incentive to stretch your capabilities with tonal variety. Do not limit your imagination merely to sounds though: imagine the smell of the concert hall – perhaps the aroma of wood, if that appeals. As you 'conduct' a great orchestra, feel pleasure in the clothes you imagine yourself to be wearing. Feel a weightlessness as you effortlessly move your arms and 'conduct' each instrument that you hear in your inner ear. You can even go as far as to 'taste' specific sounds – a chocolatey clarinet tone, or the lemon-like tangy bite of a menacing oboe flourish! Above all, feel comfortable and remember to experience deep pleasure as you role-play through your virtual performance.

In game two, you imagine yourself as a great operatic diva. When you approach a Chopin Nocturne you are literally singing, breathing and thinking from a vocal perspective. If necessary, words can be added to the melodic line (Liszt evidently wrote words over melodies on students' music).[31] Colour, direction and shaping on a small and large scale are everything here. Practice proceeds with a mixture of literal and internal singing, along with continuous attempts to emulate the vocal ideal at the keyboard itself. As in all worthy practice,

29 We can be fairly certain that Anton Schindler was fabricating his own interpretation onto Beethoven's celebrated Sonata in D minor, Op. 31 No. 2, when he claimed that the great composer said of the work: 'If you read Shakespeare's *The Tempest* you would understand the music.'
30 See *Piano Technique in Practice*, Chapter 5, for more on this, including synaesthesia.
31 For more on words in phrasing, see *Piano Technique in Practice*, 71–5.

listening remains of paramount importance, but it can be so much easier to focus on the task in hand if the atmosphere of an operatic stage is not only visualised, but actually felt.

Imagine you are in seventh heaven, floating away in the ecstatic abandon of a highly charged operatic aria! If you love the smell of lavender, breathe it in with unadulterated pleasure. Feel your favorite silk shirt next to you. Open your eyes to the beauty of the auditorium in front you. Lose awareness of time and soar ever upwards into musical infinity.

Extending the literary stimulus: interpretation as idea

One only needs to read some of Glenn Gould's writings to see how ideas, philosophical standpoints and strongly held views can influence and inspire interpretation. Such an approach to music making is often dismissed as 'intellectual' by critics, but surely there is nothing more inspiring than approaching your practice with firmly held convictions? This approach should begin and be developed away from the piano. It will not be 'dry' or cold-hearted so long as the ideas come from instinctive feelings which are nourished via emotional reactions to the music itself. As an example of ideology influencing interpretation, let's take Prokofiev's early and often criticised first sonata. It is frequently dismissed as a student piece in which the composer was uncertain of his style. But this neglected work can become so exciting if an interpretive decision is made to contrast the monumental, quasi-Anton Rubinstein octave writing, with the lyrical, poetic moments and the passages that are much more mercurial, motoric and consequently more prophetic of the mature Prokofiev to come.

Rubinstein octaves

Lyrical section

Motoric aspect

By consciously adjusting your playing from a technical and musical perspective to show the music's extremes, the work as a whole will emerge with more dramatic vibrancy. What at first appeared to be a stylistic hybrid of a sonata will re-emerge as a highly convincing and dramatically charged youthful showstopper!

Literature and music

Interpretation and involvement in the great keyboard literature is so much easier and less superficial if the player is an avid, broad and thoughtful reader. In Busoni's words, 'The musician who is only interested in music is not a musician'. Indeed, most of the great pianists and piano pedagogues of the past were widely read and had a genuine passion for culture away from their devotion to the piano. How sad then, that it is still commonplace today to find advanced students at top conservatoires who are able to perfectly execute all the runs in a Lisztian operatic paraphrase, yet have no idea of the plot of the opera which their transcription is based on, nor an awareness of the words whose melodies they are playing so accurately! Clearly even a little literary background knowledge can transform brilliant but unmemorable interpretations into something much more vibrant and convincing.

Liszt's *Paraphrase on Verdi's Rigoletto* is an excellent example. *Rigoletto* was Verdi's first big hit, and Liszt chose to base his transcription on the famous quartet 'Un di, se ben rammentomi' from Act Four of the opera. The pianism adopted by Liszt is the musical equivalent of champagne, with sparkling, bubbly scales and arpeggios adorning the tenor melody that dominates most of the piece. Quite often students are instinctively able to grasp the passionate nature of this melody with no awareness of the drama it was originally intended to be a part of. But to limit interpretation to brilliant fingerwork would be a gross misrepresentation of what Liszt was attempting to recreate.

Anyone who knows the opera will realise that the four characters involved here are singing from completely different dramatic perspectives: the tenor melody is sung by the Duke, who is attempting to seduce the contralto Maddalena, a character who finds the seduction amusing and who cannot take the Duke seriously. Meanwhile, Gilda, the soprano, is still in love with the Duke and consequently sings with wistful sadness and longing. Finally, we have the baritone, Rigoletto, who is full of revenge, even hatred, for the Duke. So here we have passion, amusement, longing and anger simultaneously, and it is surely the pianist's duty to attempt to reproduce all four strong emotions with conviction throughout the piece. In the era of YouTube, it only takes a few moments to realise this, so there is no excuse for performers not to attempt a darker bass accompaniment in emulation of the baritone whilst playing the tenor melody with rich poetry, alternating between a filigree texture (contralto) and a more intense poetic approach (soprano) for the right-hand figurations. I suggest that everyone learning this wonderful paraphrase obtains the vocal score and studies it intently, taking time to copy the words of each vocal line into the piano transcription. I also suggest much pianistic experimentation, realising the melodic threads passionately, playfully, sorrowfully and angrily in keeping with the quartet in the opera.

The great Chilean pianist Claudio Arrau once mentioned that it was 'taken for granted among Liszt's pupils' that a Faustian scenario should be applied to many of the great master's works.[32] This can readily be seen in Liszt's F minor *Transcendental Étude*, where we can label themes and figurations with different characters and aspects of Faust's character.

Example 1

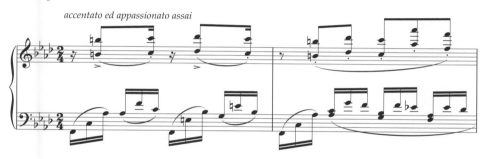

Example 2

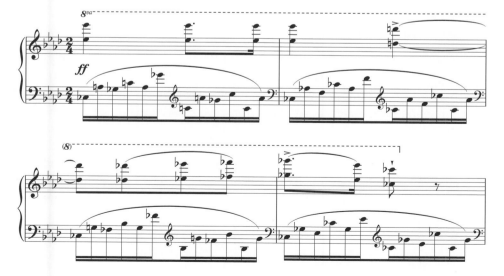

32 Joseph Horowitz, *Conversations with Arrau*, (London, 1982).

Example 3

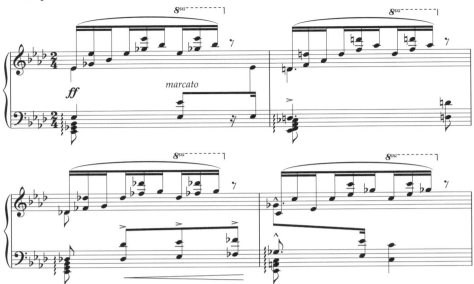

The first excerpt clearly shows a restless, troubled, searching spirit – Faust with an insatiable, almost fearful need. The second example is more passionately romantic, implying a connection with the Gretchen love scene, whilst the last is from what is possibly the most terrifying moment in the whole étude, evoking vividly a sense of eternal damnation, a casting down to hell from the Almighty Himself.

What would Liszt have made of this interpretation? Can we be sure of the authenticity of our Faustian typecasting? Ultimately it does not really matter whether or not the ideas suggested for each excerpt from Liszt's study are authentic or not. If an extra pianistic boost of inspiration from a strongly evocative literary source enhances and illuminates a young pianist's practice, then that is all that really counts.

The same is most certainly true of Liszt's great B minor Sonata. Traditionally, over the generations since Liszt's death many pianists, Claudio Arrau amongst them, have given this colossal work the full Faust treatment, working through each theme and seeing the structure in terms of Goethe's great masterpiece. In recent years, this 'Faust' interpretation has been hotly contested in certain scholarly circles, who view the sonata as a more generalised drama that pits good against evil.[33] Whether or not this new interpretation is more historically accurate is not especially interesting in terms of inspiration for the performer. What counts is the level to which the inspiration moves and affects the player. To my mind there can be no doubting the power of a 'no holds barred' Faustian approach.

---

33 See Paul Merrick 'Teufelsonate': Mephistopheles in Liszt's Piano Sonata in B minor, *The Musical TImes*, Vol. 152, No. 1914 (Spring 2011), 7–19, and 'The Devil and Liszt's sonata in B minor: Why the sonata is not a Faust work', *Piano Journal*, Issue 103, 2014, 7–14.

Octave theme

'*Mephisto*' *theme*

'*Faust*' *theme combined with* '*Mephisto*' *theme*

Some see the first theme above as an aspect of Mephisto, however I personally feel that the ambition inherent in the rising octave figurations and scales is very Faustian. By giving this theme seriousness of purpose every time it recurs, by giving emphasis on the top notes and weight to the articulation, a sense of Faust's world-weariness and dreams can be projected. The second theme is clearly a menacing, evil and sarcastic declamatory attack from Mephistopheles himself. It would be foolhardy to play this 'nicely'! On the contrary it seems to require an ugly tone in order to make a real impact. The third theme shows a terrifying combination of Mephisto in the left hand and Faust in the right (the first four notes are a variation of notes 2–4 in the right hand of the first excerpt). In this third example the pianist must attempt to use upper arm weight and elbow movements to give sonorous spaciousness to the right-hand melody notes, whilst adopting a more percussive, compact forearm and wrist technique for the left hand's repeated notes. It may be more challenging to work in these literary terms, but it is infinitely more fascinating than to work without Faustian awareness.

These principles can be adopted to fit the needs of pianists at all levels of ability and age. In *Battle Hymn of the Tiger Mother*, Amy Chua describes how her 14-year-old daughter Sophia worked at Prokofiev's *Juliet as a Young Girl* with her piano teacher, encouraging her to feel the emotional temperature of the piece in different ways.[34] The right-hand melody of the transcription should be played beautifully, but with a purity of tone and a straightforward sense of phrasing to reflect the 'coolness' of Juliet's character; though she knows she is desirable and beautiful, Juliet also feels embarrassed and flattered by the attention that Romeo (a somewhat older, more experienced character) is giving her. Later in the same piece, Romeo's theme needs a richer, deeper tonal palette to project his totally different character and his greater experience of life. This approach needs to be complemented by an awareness of which instruments are playing in the original orchestral score. Simply put, it is never enough to simply play all the notes in the correct order.

It is impossible to do too much visualisation away from the piano. Indeed, you can view every activity of your life as 'piano practice' from a certain perspective. It is not simply a matter of preparing individual works for performance in your head. It goes much further than background research, whether that is reading books associated with a particular composer or composition, or taking time to look at masterpieces of art, plays, ballets, operas or whatever. In its macro-state, practising the piano is a 24/7 activity. After all, the quality and quantity of sleep, food, exercise, socialising and thinking you do all directly affects your piano playing, whether you like to admit that fact or not. So, when someone asks the inevitable question 'How much piano practice do you do each day?' the only truthful answer to give in response is 'I never stop practising!' How you organise your practising is a much more complicated matter. It takes great discipline to structure things so that you have a good balance in terms of what you do, whether that is at the piano or away from it.

34 Amy Chua, *Battle Hymn of the Tiger Mother*, (Penguin, 2011).

8 Talent, musicality and emotional involvement

Talent

How can you tell if someone is talented? How much is down to nature and how much is due to nurture? Evaluating musical talent will always be a subjective and controversial endeavor, because 'talent' is extremely hard to define. Certainly, there are many different kinds of talents; it could well be argued that it takes just as much talent to have tenacity and organisational powers in practice as it does to memorise music quickly and securely. And in any case, is talent teachable? Do we take an idealistic approach and say 'yes', or should we be realistic and concede that there are certain things in the biological and psychological make-up of humanity that are given by genetics which simply cannot be altered? Are pianists fixed with a proverbial musical IQ from day one and stuck with it for the rest of their lives? Is there a 'threshold' of achievement?

These questions are riddled with danger. To create a proverbial 'Richter Talent Scale' for musicians from their earliest years, with the highest ranked pinpointed for special 'musical earthquakes' later in their careers, is potentially to demotivate all those who are not ranked at the top, as well as to risk being grossly unfair to 'winners', placing too much responsibility on their shoulders.[35] Quite apart from anything else, it is severely patronising and authoritarian to imply that talent is a fixed phenomenon. We should always feel that people can change, and that there should be no such thing as a threshold of achievement. 'Everything is possible if you want it to be' is a very healthy starting point.

An all-star society

Though we cannot all be stars, we can all certainly twinkle! Claudio Arrau once mentioned that 'even the smallest talent is special'. We would do well to remember that, and to constantly realise that human potential, if developed and encouraged with emotional intelligence and love, is unlimited. We also need to remember that life is about the journey, not the destination. And it certainly isn't about the start either. At birth we are all endowed with different attributes and abilities – some of us have large hands, some small; certain students pick up sight-reading more quickly than others; some seem more adept at performing in concerts than in exams, and vice versa. Whatever your pluses and (apparent) minuses, take time to celebrate them. For all musicians, the joys of learning and discovery far outweigh what nature and fate has bestowed on us.

---

35 Of course, it all comes down to how teachers, parents and institutions treat those in their care. Certainly, it is wrong to make anyone feel dismissed or 'classified' as 'of average talent' or 'unexceptional ability'.

There has never been a better era for aspiring pianists than the early 21st century! The international piano community is living in an age of optimistic possibility. So much of what used to be thought unmanageable, unpractical or unrealistic is now very much a reality. There are more solutions and strategies for helping pianists of all levels than ever before. To give but a few examples: those with small hands can now consider using smaller keyboards, as manufactured by Steinbuhler. This means that the bigger repertoire can now be tackled by more players. Pianists with dyslexia and reading difficulties have more support and guidance than ever before. Medicine has made quantum leaps forward, meaning that musicians are now being understood and catered for to a far greater extent whenever they encounter physical difficulties. Mindfulness and music therapy continue to develop beyond levels ever thought imaginable. There are now structured and balanced courses and approaches for musicians who suffer from tension and anxiety. Pianists who struggle to memorise are no longer shunned in the way they often used to be in certain circles. It is becoming increasingly common to witness professional pianists reading scores from iPads, which are operated by the use of a mouse on the floor next to the pedals of the piano! In terms of pedagogy as a whole, this century so far has seen an enormous growth in the adult amateur sector, with far more over-30s returning or starting music lessons than was ever the case pre-2000. And we are becoming less narrow-minded in terms of our understanding of technique. Pioneering teachers such as Philip Fowke, understand the frustrations, misery and lack of success that can come from approaching specific technical problems that pupils may face if they always follow the text in a literal sense. By subtle rearrangement, the sensitive omission of only a few notes here and there, and lots of lateral thinking, Fowke in his lecture 'To cheat or not to cheat, that is the question!', has shown that it is possible to achieve convincing musical results for particular technical 'nasties' that would otherwise place lots of repertoire completely beyond the scope of many players.[36] Puritans and traditionalists may roll in their graves but the 21st century seems set to prove that in all kinds of ways the impossible really can be achieved!

Musicality

What about artistry? What makes one pianist or one performance seem more 'musical' than another? Can you cultivate genius? Is it possible to teach or acquire sensitivity and communication, or is the 'X factor' something that you are either born with or not? We all know when we have heard something artistically special and magical from even the most inexperienced of players in the most modest of pieces.

36 As outlined by Fowke in an inspiring lecture with that title given at Chetham's Summer School and Festival for Pianists (www.pianosummerschool.com and elsewhere).

The opening of Bach's first two-part Invention serves as a good illustration. Executed dispassionately these bars can appear objective and academic. Let's imagine a young pianist playing this opening – a conscientious student who has worked hard and can play accurately, but who somehow just cannot engage us as listeners. What makes one performance of this piece more emotionally engaged than another?

Let's imagine that our worthy young pianist has chosen a speed that is good and that beautiful tone is evident throughout. Let's also assume that there is tasteful ornamentation, stylistic awareness, clarity of fingerwork and a steady pulse. In a scenario like this one, we need to go beyond the notes to find star quality and magic. In no particular order, here is a list of some of the traditional approaches that teachers often use to encourage heightened expressivity and a communicative interpretation.

1 Shading

As the music rises and falls it makes sense to experiment with 'hairpin' *crescendos* and *diminuendos*. We naturally do this when we speak enthusiastically or sing. To sing or talk with a consistently monochrome tone is clearly unattractive, and the same goes for piano playing. On the other hand, too much 'shading' can become unsubtle, predictable or rather manic. Successful tonal colouring occurs when the player is sensitive enough to project minute variations in dynamics with natural ease; play it as you would sing it and you should not go wrong!

2 Articulation

This music presents a blank canvas and it is up to the performer to create convincing *staccatos*, slurs and shapes. Ask a violinist to add bow markings to each line of music, then try to emulate the bowing via accentuation, note groupings and tapered phrase endings. Alternatively, ask a woodwind player to show you where s/he would breathe in the music. You should have a much clearer awareness of the phrase units as a result.

3 Texture

Piano playing requires an awareness of tonal balance. In order to play with conviction, you need to be able to multitask and cope with more than one voice at a time. In this passage the response of the left hand to the right is crucial and it is vital that you set up a dialogue between the hands from the first bar. Really feel that there are human voices engaged in exchanges as you play.

Always isolate the left-hand part in your practising so that it gains at least the same amount of importance as the right. Immediate interpretive enrichment can be achieved simply by projecting the lower voices to a greater extent in every bar.

4 *Phrase structure*

Music is a language; we have commas, sentences, paragraphs and whole essays. Find climaxes, mini-climaxes, pauses for breath, explanation marks and expletives in all of your music, ensuring that your music making is delivered in a language that everyone will understand. Sometimes it can be useful to make up words and sing or say them under each note. This was done by the 19th century musicologist Ebenezer Prout for all of the Bach '48' Fugue subjects.[37] Whilst amusing and diverting on one level, if Prout's approach encourages greater energy in the delivery of musical shape, then its importance cannot be over-stated.

5 *Rubato*

The ability to play in time is an essential framework for interpretation at every level. However, musicians need to be able to feel the space between the notes, and to articulate expressivity through subtle, sensitive rhythmic variations and changes. Examples of this can be seen in the Bach excerpt below. Look in the right hand at the rising perfect fourth (G–C) in bar 1 and the descending fifth (D–G) in bar 2. Both these intervals require more time from the performer than the space needed between the scale notes that surround them. Feeling and projecting miniscule differences in rhythm is part and parcel of connecting to the music. Intellectually expressive moments on the text can be shown to students, but ultimately it needs to be felt physically. It can help to choreograph a piece through physical gesture and movement. Conducting an imaginary orchestra is a useful means of finding out just how much *accelerando* and *ritardando* is required within a given pulse.

Desire

What is it that makes one pianist sound as though s/he has been 'taught' musicality and another sound totally natural? Why does one pianist's interpretation appear manufactured whilst another's seems truthful? We have all heard manufactured *rubato*, phrasing, voicing, colours, and characterisation and cringed as a result. Perhaps this is the crux of the nature versus nurture discussion. For an answer, we need to look at the pianist's concentration, focus and, above all, commitment. If there is any suspicion that a particular pianist may not be quite as involved in his/her playing as could be the case, then this will be detected in every phrase that is heard. Perhaps it is this deep inner compulsion, this strong commitment that all great artists apparently possess in one form or another, that just cannot be taught. It is only in the context of

37   Ebenezer Prout, *Analysis of J.S. Bach's Forty-Eight Fugues* (Das wohltemperirte clavier) (Edwin Ashdown, 1910).

desire that I would ever use the old saying 'You can lead a horse to water but you can't make him drink'. When it comes to ingrained emotions and will-power, people, like horses, will only do what they have a real lust to do.

Feeling

'Depth of feeling would seem to imply a complete absorption in the given mood. If you remain morose or merely indifferent while the carnival swirls around you, if you fail to be affected, moved by the satirical masks, the power of misrule, the vengeful wit run riot, then you are incapable of sounding the depths of feeling.'[38]

Ferruccio Busoni

Desire is certainly fuelled by strong intensity. Intensity and power of concentration are essential for charisma, star quality, and transcendental 'peak experience' in performance. Teachers often express frustrations when trying to help introverted musicians to express feelings that they may well have strongly within them for the music they are performing, but which they seem incapable of projecting. It can be hard work when you are dealing with shyness. How to release inhibitions so that emotions and expressions can be projected with confidence and authority? Too often shy people can be wrongly labelled as 'intellectual', cerebral or simply unemotional musicians. Experience over the years with talented but introverted pupils has shown that this is often far from true. In many cases it is because introverts care and feel so much for the music they are playing that they get into trouble with their emotions in the first place. The responsibility of projecting everything as truthfully as possible becomes an almost overwhelming weight, preventing the lightness of spirit necessary to let go and allow the music's own energy to take flight.

Happily, there are techniques which can be practised and specifically developed to ensure that introverted performers are able to let go and allow their music making to speak for itself. Here are some of the 'trigger' techniques and activities which have proved successful with numerous students in need of emotional release.

Shouting and screaming

In a society where conformity and containment is expected in many day to day situations, it can be challenging to let one's guard down within a classical piano piece. In so many cases budding pianists seem unable to unbutton and 'let rip' in the way they need to if their *Mephisto Waltz* or *Heroic Polonaise* is going to convince.

Go out into the great outdoors on your own and ideally stand on a hill or at least an isolated raised area in a park, and literally scream at the top of your voice. Enjoy your emotions! Let go and see how powerful you can become vocally. When you are convinced that you have indeed given your all at the

38 Ferruccio Busoni, *Sketch of a New Esthetic of Music* (Schirmer, 1907).

top of your range, take time to remember how you felt. Ideally there should be a sense of relaxed strength, ease and egoless laissez-faire about the whole experience. You can then emulate these attributes in the biggest climaxes of your repertoire. If you do this on more than a few occasions you should find that the experience gives you the confidence to relax and become even more ferociously committed to musical assignments.

Adrenalin

There is a famous anecdote about Percy Grainger and the Grieg Concerto at the Royal Albert Hall in London. Evidently, he ran all the way round the building before dashing onto stage to give an exhilarating performance, much to the astonishment of onlookers. In fact, by releasing so much physical energy before playing Grainger was using adrenalin to exorcise performance anxiety and the unhelpful negativity that can accompany this. We can all learn from Grainger in this respect and include cardiovascular exercise as a regular part of our practice. Whether or not performers choose to always go for a manic sprint five minutes before a concert is more of an open question!

Apart from all of the health benefits of physical activity, it unquestionably encourages the development of a stronger connection between mind and body. Too many pianists tend to look self-conscious and disconnected at the instrument. It is as though they have ceased to be aware of how they actually move physically! Exercise and good health promote a real mind-body-soul connection, so ensuring a sense of oneness – an organic flow from motivation to intention. This can most clearly be seen in the way pianists sit at the piano, as well as in their movements.

Laugh, dance and sing!

In our quest to express ourselves freely we would do well to remember Charlie Chaplin's belief that 'a day without laughter is a day wasted', as well as Kabalevsky's assertion that all of his music could be classified as being a 'march, song or dance'. Nothing beats the pleasure, release and physical exhilaration of extended laughter. 'Letting go' regularly for some downtime giggles will not only keep life in a healthy perspective, but also allow you to relax into yourself as a person. Posture, emotional perspective and physical comfort are all enhanced quickly and effectively when you allow yourself to be moved by a joke or two.

Singing and dancing can be just as enjoyable, if not quite as uncontrollable, as laughter. If you cannot take time out to stomp around the room in time to your repertoire, liltingly swirl as you hum the main melodic thread of your Beethoven first movement (ideally with a few impulsive giggles along the way), then you are missing out on a lot of pleasurable activity as well as psychological development as a musician. Never lose your childish naivety and grace – to do so is to cripple your creativity and restrict your sense of abandon.

'The eyes are the windows to the soul'

Many actors and singers begin to develop communicative projection by considering how they use (or do not use) their eyes. We can certainly open out considerably in a natural way by allowing our eyes to project emotions as we play. Before doing this, it is worth taking time out from the piano studio to stand in front of a mirror and 'act out' emotional reactions to various feelings. It should be possible, with practice, to project all emotional feelings convincingly using nothing but your eyes. As you develop this you will find that your facial muscles begin to copy your eyes. It will not be difficult to move your arms and your upper torso in keeping with the sentiments your eyes are projecting.

Returning to the piano, it can be illuminating to read some music through entirely without playing a note, but 'playing' the emotions of the piece with your eyes. Perhaps this is best done at first with a selection of short, moderately easy pieces from an anthology such as Schumann's *Album for the Young*. You could try and project heroic strength in the outer sections of 'Knight Rupert' with your eyes fully opened. Feel them glowing and vibrant in keeping with the exciting textures. In the central section, calmness prevails. Your eyes can relax and feel more restful. In 'The Merry Peasant' you can project a gentle sense of coquettish charm for the most part whilst in 'Winter' you can adopt a more mournful, sorrowful gaze.

This can be tremendous fun, but it is also a very strong method of empowering conviction and authority in your inner approach. Many years ago, I spent an entire afternoon practising the whole of Rachmaninov's Second Piano Concerto in this manner, and felt significantly more focused, inspired and 'prepared' in an emotional sense as a result.

Movement

A pianist's physical gestures and facial expressions tend not to be noticed by onlookers if they are truly natural and sincere. Starting with our eyes, work with your instinctive and immediate emotional responses to particular phrases and see where that leads you in terms of physicality. If you are sincerely engaged in characterisation – which comes from your direct feelings about the music in question – you may well find that you naturally start to move about a little as you play. When you have flowing arpeggios, it seems perfectly natural to move your body from side to side, or in swirling gestures.

Natural physical movements may well expand and develop as you steep yourself in your practising. And when it comes to concerts, the desire to communicate with others may magnify gestures to an even greater extent. This will only feel comfortable to audiences if there is a really organic unity of purpose – if the gestures are not seen as 'add-ons' put in place to try and impress. In the worst scenario, grimacing, swinging from side to side and gesticulating seem to be put in place by pianists to hide a lack of interpretive commitment. In these sad cases, it is as though the performer has little to say with the piano itself, so substitutes a visual distraction instead.

In conclusion, it is fair to say that gestures and facial expressions are only negative when they distract from the prime consideration on stage and in the practice studio, which is unquestionably the music that is being performed, and not the pianist!

Controlling your emotions

After practising eye exercises and projecting emotions with appropriate body movements, it is important to learn how to bring control into the picture. Do not let the physical manifestations of emotional reactions come into play as you perform. To do so is to lose the ability to control your body. Technical consistency depends on sophisticated discipline. You need to contain within yourself all your tears, sweat, emotional turmoil and angst. You can, indeed you must, be receptive to all the emotions that come to you via your repertoire as you play it, but you cannot relinquish your role as master over them. By all means break down into sobbing spasms after a performance, but whilst actually playing, your emotions need to be contained within you. Think of them as simmering sensations just under the boil, which are contained in your body to the very surface of your skin. As a performing artist, you will certainly have a real awareness of emotional excitement as you play, but you can never turn up the excitement to full boil. If they spill out during a performance then you will be unable to project your interpretations with technical authority. There will be unpredictability and insecurity.

Harnessing your emotions in a disciplined, professional way can be mistaken for emotional detachment. This is quite different from the emotional control suggested here. When refined and realised to a sophisticated state, emotional control means that a performer can remain the most reserved looking individual in a concert hall. The auditorium may be a sobbing, throbbing mass of emotional hysteria and turmoil, but the performing artist has to retain a surface serenity. This is brilliantly alluded to by Busoni in his 'New Aesthetic' essay when he says, 'In life, we are accustomed to expressions of feeling, conveyed in gestures or in words; much rarer, and more genuine, is the kind of feeling that is communicated without speaking, and most precious of all is the feeling that is concealed'.[39]

39 Ibid.

Part 3
Development and health

The piano and its literature provide a cultural inheritance that is dynamic, kinetic and open to constant reappraisal. Pianists must remain relaxed, vibrant and healthy if they are to continue to develop positively and creatively.

9 Methodology and strategic planning

> 'Though this be madness, yet there is method in it.'
>
> William Shakespeare, *Hamlet*, Act 2, Scene 9

The spirit of music is too magical and precious to be bound by any dogmatism or systematic formulae. As soon as artists become rigid, predictable or intolerant of exceptions, then they are on a sliding scale towards mediocrity. In short, they cease to be artists and metamorphose into pedants. It is interesting to remember that disciples of Leschetitzky, surely one of the most important piano pedagogues of all time, were on very slippery ground in teaching 'The Leschetitzky Method' since the great master himself always said that he never had a 'method' as such![40]

Fundamentals of musicianship

It is still vital for pianists to have fundamental musical and technical principles as discussed in this book and its two predecessors, *The Foundations of Technique* and *Piano Technique in Practice*. From the first lesson – or ideally before it – pianists should begin to develop a strong awareness of rhythm and pitch via clapping and singing. Singing can be one of the greatest joys in a child's life, and ideally it should remain a joy in adulthood too. As pianists, we should never lose sight of the fact that so many of our 'inner conceptions' for phrasing, beauty and creativity come from the human voice. This should lead naturally and inevitably into a lifelong desire to produce the most beautiful sounds possible at the piano. Rhythmic coordination can be improved by daily exercises (Hindemith's book *Elementary training for young musicians* is still very useful in the 21st century) whilst the solfège approach as recommended by Kodály is still one of the best ways to instil a strong sense of pitch awareness. Kodály, Orff and Dalcroze still remain amongst the most important and inspiring of pedagogical approaches for the strongest possible grounding in rhythm and pitch. We could do much worse than to embrace fully their values and beliefs.

Posture and basic technique

It is saddening to note that so many young players start off so well, only to degenerate into rounded shoulders, stooped backs, stiff wrists and general tension later. The fact that virtually all under-fives can sit so well at the piano should be a warning for later on. It is therefore essential to consistently develop

40   See *Piano Technique in Practice*, 164–7.

and nurture an organic ease and a natural approach to the sitting at the keyboard. We should strive for a sense of oneness with the instrument. As has been emphasised throughout *The Foundations of Technique*, the concept of having loose wrists simultaneously with 'fingers of steel' summarises so much of the demands expected for authoritative playing. This should be a top consideration throughout your piano playing career.

Programmes of study

Virtually every professional at work in modern society has to be subject to accountability via appraisals, work plans, records, syllabus guidelines and so on. It therefore follows that pianists also need 'road maps' to function both as long term programmes of study and routes which can be used to rebel against from time to time. In short, we need to have a 'system' in our work at the piano guarding against a descent into a blind pedantry which would make us sterile and uninspiring!

Unless we are extremely diligent, the dangerous temptation is to stick to a 'rulebook' and squeeze all of the talent which comes our way into the same repertoire, exercises, attitudes and career paths as though we were human sausage machines.

Surely the answer, for teachers at least, is to nurture each and every pupil as a totally unique talent. Every pianist on the planet has different strengths, weaknesses and interests. An ideal programme of study would account for this wonderful diversity whilst also ensuring that each aspect of technique is covered. It would need to embrace the basics, ensuring that musical, mechanical, technical, imaginative, rhythmic, intellectual, emotional and psychological principles are set up and developed.

Scales, arpeggios and broken chords

Scales can be extended in order to develop not only stamina but also velocity, strength, tone production and coordination.[41] Try different ways to gradually increase the level of difficulty: mix articulation, try different dynamics between the hands, play scales with crossed hands or with your eyes shut, begin on different degrees of the scale, make the hands play in different keys. Work your way up a graded exam syllabus by all means, but never feel that you have exhausted all permutations for scales – it is just not possible!

Exercises

In planning out a course of technical development, we could do worse than follow the guidelines set up in the 19th and early 20th centuries by famous pianists in their collections of exercises. The thorough approaches of Hanon, Beringer, Dohnanyi, Tankard and Harrison, and Schmitt (to mention but a few names) have stood the test of time. In the UK, young pianists have been

---

41   These ideas are also discussed in *Piano Technique in Practice*, ibid.

nurtured successfully from the earliest stages by the series of exercises under the title *A dozen a day*,[42] as well as by Joan Last's sensitive course entitled *Freedom in piano technique*.[43] At a later stage in development, the exercises of Brahms and Cortot are invaluable.

Studies

Piano études are of the utmost importance in building up a player's technique. They can begin with tried and trusted favourites by such composers as Heller and Burgmüller before Czerny is introduced. In South Korea in particular, certain teachers follow what is referred to as a 'Czerny ladder'. Starting with Czerny's easiest eight-bar studies (for instance the 101 *exercises*, Op.261) it steps towards *The School of Velocity*, Op.299, before reaching the heights of *The Art of Finger Dexterity*, Op.740, and beyond! In total, there are well over a thousand Czerny études to choose from! Some of them have ferociously hard mechanical demands – it is not for nothing that Sergei Rachmaninov reputedly still practised *The Art of Finger Dexterity* when at the height of his powers.

The studies of Chopin remain amongst the most challenging and significant transcendental peaks of the piano repertoire. Virtually every pianist must practise them at some stage in their development. Perhaps they are best introduced to most pianists once they can manage about half a dozen of Czerny's Op.740. Studies by Liszt, Rachmaninov, Debussy, Scriabin then Prokofiev, Alkan, Ligeti, Bartók and many others can then follow as taste, individual preference and circumstances dictate.

Three piece syndrome

One of the major issues amateur players of all ages face is that of limited repertoire. In the UK, this can be blamed, at least in part, on an unhealthy exclusive musical diet of grade examinations. Sadly, an all too common culture has developed over the generations whereby children learning the piano are given a programme of work which allows for a complete academic year to pass in preparation for entering a grade exam. We have already discussed exams in Chapter 4. They were never designed as piano courses. If they become the only musical aim in a pianist's life then a 'three piece only' framework is set up, which is extremely harmful and counterproductive. In the classic scenario a player would work obsessively hard on these pieces, perform them once in front of an examiner, audience or masterclass tutor, then immediately stop playing them. They would then move onto another collection of (three) pieces and repeat the process. By the time the new pieces are ready to be performed, the old pieces are out of the system and too unfamiliar to be performed without lots of hard work. Inevitably the prospect of a hard slog is unappealing, simply because there is less enthusiasm to work on music that has already had lots of practice time spent on it, and the old repertoire is therefore never

42 Edna-Mae Burnam, *A dozen a day*, (The Willis Music Company, 1950).
43 Joan Last, *Freedom in piano technique*, (Oxford University Press, 1971).

relearnt. Players in this all too familiar situation then often choose to learn some new music instead. This means that they are repeating the same pattern and, sadly, failing to expand and build up a repertoire of anything more than three pieces at any one given time.

If you are only working on three pieces for a whole year, then you will inevitably over-practice them and lose a sense of perspective. This tends to involve playing through repertoire for psychological reassurance rather than for any other reason. Such an approach ultimately leads to boredom and negativity – if you are playing rather than practising, inevitably you will eventually lose interest. Dislike of the music will increase strongly on a daily basis.

Even away from the grade exam culture, many pianists find that they flounder if they focus on more than several pieces at any given time. Inexperienced players will not progress if they spread their wings too broadly and end up with a wide-ranging but completely approximate repertoire. Even you only need an exclusive focus on two or three pieces for a couple of months at a time, a lack of sparkle and a sense of déja-vous can all too easily lead to apathy and dejection.

Keeping it fresh

So, what is the answer? Is it possible to work at length with an intense and purposeful approach on a small number of notes without becoming completely disillusioned in the process? Happily, my answer is unequivocally 'yes'! Let's explore ways in which you can retain freshness, creativity, interest and focus with only a couple of pieces in your daily practice regime at any given time.

We have already mentioned how important it is to avoid simply playing through your pieces at practice time. Start from the premise that when practising you are trying to avoid the piece sounding recognisable to anyone who may happen to overhear you. If you do this, you cannot fail! Take small sections at a time for this 'game'. Of course, it can be played by pianists at all levels, including professional performers. If you are practising with focus on specific issues such as position shifts, connections between individual notes, fingerings and articulation, then there should be no need to play with anything other than bite-sized fragments at a time. Experience has shown that the most effective practice comes from working in these micro-sized chunks of music. How sad then that for purely psychological reasons, many inexperienced players persist in practising in large sections, skimming over many different problems and issues when they could so easily focus on successfully improving just one jump, fingering, voicing or technical manoeuvre at a time.

For those who have over-indulged in 'play-throughs' when they should have been practising, this exercise may feel similar to going on an extreme diet. By starving yourself of performing your pieces you will develop a longing for playing them. This is extremely healthy as it energises and empowers enthusiasm for your working repertoire.

Try at least one mental performance of each piece you are working at every day. The technique of playing through repertoire in your head away from the piano has been discussed in Chapter 7, and its importance for motivation and psychological focus cannot be over-stated. When you do return to practising out loud, make the conservation of energy a top priority. By that I mean avoid working at optimum speed and dynamic levels for the most part.

Slow and quiet practice focuses the brain and makes it possible to work for longer stretches at a time. It also makes it possible for you to be more aware and precise, simply because you are working well within your physical limits and so have the time to notice much more than when you are stressed and mechanically challenged.

When you do feel the urge for more kinetic activity at the keyboard, never forget that piano playing is most creative and stimulating when it is approached in a lateral-minded way (see Chapter 6). Do not stand still or be predicable. Experiment constantly with different dynamics, tempos and articulation markings. Make up words for the melody line. Sing the tune whilst playing the accompaniment. Try dancing round the room in time to the piece. Or if that is too embarrassing, try conducting instead. Make up little 'étudettes' or improvisatory flourishes based on your favourite parts of your repertoire. Try transposing selected phrases into nearby keys. In the example below (the opening two bars of C.P.E. Bach's most famous keyboard piece, his *Solfeggietto*) it can be technically empowering, as well as artistically stimulating, to practise it with at least four different articulations:

1 *Slur four semiquavers for each beat*

2 *Slur the first two notes in each beat, and make the third and fourth semiquavers staccato*

3 *Slur the first three notes in each beat, and make the fourth note staccato*

4 *Make the first note in each bar staccato, and slur the second, third and fourth notes*

Moving away from a small repertoire: weekly 'play-throughs'

The simple way out of 'three-piece syndrome' is to set aside a period each week in which you play through your entire repertoire. I am reminded of an old gentleman passenger I met years ago, when performing recitals on the QE2. Every day as I came to practise on the ship's piano he was finishing off his daily run-through of repertoire – and he was fairly dazzling for an amateur player, making a pretty decent job of Liszt's *Liebestraum*, Debussy's *Clair de lune* and up to a dozen or so other 'lollipops'. When I asked him to sight-read through some duets with me for fun, he laughed and told me that he could hardly read music at all; he had been a child prodigy pianist in New York and every note I heard from his restricted repertoire of about 15 works had been learnt before he was 13 years of age. He did not wish to lose what he had gained working as a kid, so had a daily routine of playing through his repertoire over a three-day cycle – a practice routine that he had lovingly cultivated for over 30 years!

But how do you choose music to expand your repertoire? The piano has been blessed with a bigger range of music than any other instrument, and this sheer quantity is daunting in itself. With such a large amount on offer, it seems sensible to choose music that suits your own personality, hand-size and interests. It is nearly always unwise to pick music that you feel is good for you, but which privately you do not particularly like. To prepare music to a level of performance requires hours and hours of work, and there are few things more dispiriting in life than living with music you do not warm to for that amount of time in your practice slots. So, do not allow yourselves to be bullied into choices favoured by teachers, friends or fellow pianists. Wise mentors always allow their protégées an element of freedom when it comes to repertoire selection. Give yourself ample opportunity to do research and take an active interest in what players of your own level decide to take up. This is where attending summer schools, courses and piano groups can be especially valuable and inspiring. There is so much more to piano study than simply sitting at your instrument and slogging out reams of notes on a regular basis. Do get out there and explore the pianist's paradise via public concerts, chats, browsing sessions in good quality sheet music retailers and so on! When you are choosing new material to play, don't limit your choice by staying exclusively mainstream. There are literally thousands of undiscovered or under-played jewels in the piano repertoire, and it can be very rewarding to find and perform them. Bring logic and continuity to your exploration of repertoire by finding rarities similar to works you have already prepared. For example, if you have learnt and enjoyed Beethoven's *Für Elise* then why not try the first movement of Kuhlau's Sonata in A minor, which begins in an almost identical way before branching into new directions? And if you enjoy Satie's *Gymnopedies* or *Gnossiennes* then do look out for Maltese unsung hero Charles Camilleri and his exquisite *Due Cantilena* (published by Roberton).

Repertoire road maps

In terms of repertoire development one could do much worse than look at the road maps created by the likes of Bach, Mozart, Schumann, Kabalevsky and Bartók. I am a firm believer in building blocks and systematic progress with regard not only to technique but also to expanding your interpretive horizons. Everyone should have at least some experience of J.S. Bach's *Anna Magdalena Bach Notebook*. After learning some of the Menuets in this celebrated collection, follow with work on the two-part Inventions, then the three-part Inventions (sinfonias) followed by the 48 Preludes and Fugues (*The Well-Tempered Clavier*, Books One and Two) and finally movements from *The Art of Fugue*. You do not need to learn every single piece in all of these collections but it is important to learn more than one or two before progressing to the next set. It is interesting to see what happens when you learn more than one piece in a similar style and of a similar technical level – your brain makes connections and links new pieces with patterns and similarities already encountered. This makes the learning process much quicker and ultimately much more pleasurable. Self-esteem is so important in developing piano playing, and if you are constantly learning music that is on the very threshold of your technical ability, then you will never feel at ease in your practice time. I strongly advise players to build on the triumph of successfully performing Bach's C major two-part Invention by continuing with one of the others (let's pick the F major piece for the sake of argument) and then the A minor number from the same collection. There are students who will feel impatient and who would rather jump from one anthology to the more difficult one without pausing for breath. These characters are very similar to children who are pushed from one grade exam directly into the next by misguided parents and teachers. Ultimately it leaves the player bereft of musical background, understanding and enjoyment.

Before moving on, it is probably a good idea to list some of the other piano road maps created by celebrated composers. In the case of Robert Schumann, it is a pleasure for adult amateurs and young children alike to begin with his exquisite *Album for the Young*, before moving forward with *Scenes of Childhood* and *Forest Scenes* before embarking on the demands of *Papillons*, then the *Abegg Variations* and finally blockbuster warhorses such as *Carnaval*, the C major Fantasy and *Kriesleriana*. Both Mozart and Tchaikovsky produced charming miniatures for younger players (many of the Mozartian examples were penned before the age of ten, albeit with help from Dad), and these lead naturally into more extended sonatas and pieces (such as Tchaikovsky's suite, *The seasons*). Many of the Soviet composers produced children's pieces which provide excellent stimulation and preparation for the great sonatas in the 20th century repertoire by the likes of Prokofiev and Shostakovich. Perhaps Kabalevsky deserves special mention here, as he wrote well over a hundred miniatures for younger players, many of which can sound utterly charming when performed by professional players. It makes sense to work through groups of Kabalevsky pieces, as they are of variable difficulty and lead naturally into his charming sonatinas. Work can then commence on his 'Youth' Piano Concerto No.3, his impressively crafted, dramatic and humorous third sonata, and even his rarely heard second sonata and remarkable set of 24 Preludes based on Russian folksong.

Of course, the most systematic composer of the 20th century in terms of pianistic development remains Bartók. Not only did he write wonderful children's piano miniatures, he also compiled the extraordinary collection of well over 100 piano pieces in six volumes entitled *Mikrokosmos* which takes the player from pre-grade one level up to concert standard. This is not only an excellent way of building up your repertoire and technique simultaneously, but also a marvellous course in compositional technique and analysis for the general musician.

A set of keys: opening doors for all the repertoire

The really astute teacher will develop a player's repertoire by making sure that the core fundamentals of technique for each of the classical piano styles are in place. Though the piano repertoire is colossal, there are only a few basic 'keys' necessary for success. Let's look at each one in turn:

1 Bach counterpoint: The ability to separate voices in textures clearly is an invaluable skill and will open doors not only for the baroque repertoire, but for music where it is essential to show different textures and layers of sound. Music from Bach through to the present day requires this skill.

2 'Mozartian' clarity: This is primarily achieved through precise articulation and excellent finger independence, but it also demands control, dexterity, *leggiero* and an effervescence in sound quality and phrasing in the full gamut of dynamics, with minimum use of the pedals.

3 'Beethovenian' strength: Structural clarity, finger-strength, lucidity, projection and infallible rhythm are necessary if you wish to play Beethoven

(and indeed many a sonata from other periods). For this reason, it is important not to neglect Beethoven as you develop your playing. The bagatelles can and indeed should be introduced to players from about grade five onwards and they lead naturally into the sonata movements (Op.49 Nos. 1 and 2 followed by the pre-Op.2 sonatas, the Op.14 pair and so on).

4 'Chopinesque' sensitivity: It takes lots of searching to play with seamless *legatissimo*, to control shading, pedalling, voicing and *rubato* in a deeply tasteful yet quintessentially romantic way. It is most obviously worth cultivating if you wish to add not only Chopin's cornerstone works to your repertoire, but also the music of all the romantics from Schubert and Mendelssohn upwards.

5 'Lisztian' virtuosity: Learn to barnstorm and project as a powerhouse pianist and you will be able to tackle transcendental études, Soviet sonatas and bravura concertos! Obviously, this repertoire is not for everyone, but it is helpful at least to begin nurturing the kind of technical tools you would need to be a Rach. 3 'big shooter': double octaves, thick chords, projection, stamina, brilliance and superhuman memory. Where to start? Well, all of these techniques are at least touched upon in basic technical exercises by the likes of Hanon, Beringer and Brahms (in his 51 exercises) and they are extended almost to breaking point in Liszt's *Paganini* and *Transcendental Études*. If you want a taster of this quality of pianism that is a little more manageable, then a good starting point could be the simplified versions of the *Transcendental Études* that Liszt composed prior to his definitive versions (still widely available).

6 'Debussian' colour: Debussy's extraordinary music requires extraordinary colours, articulation, control and attention to detail. The Debussy sound was totally iconoclastic in his period and remains an extraordinary challenge for pianists today. Begin with the early works (*Deux Arabesques*, *Valse Romantique* etc.), keep going via the suites, and you will nourish your tonal palette to a vibrant extent.

7 20th century percussion: Works such as Bartók's *Allegro Barbaro* and Prokofiev's *Suggestion Diabolique* brought a new motoric and percussive edge to pianism that had never been heard before. Being able to articulate with razor-edged brilliance and clarity is an essential skill for those who wish to tackle Copland, Stravinsky et al. Working through Bartók's 'educational' pieces will certainly help, especially as the easiest of these are well below the grade five mark (e.g. *For Children* and the first two volumes of *Mikrokosmos*).

How to maintain and develop a large repertoire

1 Set aside a weekly slot for playing through your entire repertoire.

2 Always learn at least a few pieces that are well within your technical ability.

3 For rapid repertoire expansion, learn new pieces that have something in common stylistically and technically with those you have recently mastered.

4 Collect a recorded anthology of your performances.

5 Understand the different challenges and needs required in order to play music by different composers from each stylistic period.

10 Tactics for daily development

Are your daily habits toxic to your brain's health?

Harmful	Helpful
Tied to technologies	Brain downtime
Multitasking	Sequential tasking
Information overload	Prioritising
Cruising on autopilot	Innovation

Having discussed love, inspiration and strategies for long-term organisation, let's now focus on how to sustain creativity and motivation on a daily basis. Techniques, approaches and ideas are needed that will enable us to continue maximising both our enjoyment and our development as pianists, even when there appears to be very little time available in our lives to practise. We need tactics to strengthen ourselves so that we can remain focused and tackle any potential distractions that may occur as the going gets tough.

How to conquer daily demons and remain a steadfast practiser

Everyone knows how excited and energised life at the piano can be after an inspirational lesson, an exciting recital we have attended, or simply a fresh start at some new repertoire. After a boost of musical stimuli, we have a renewed purpose giving us a sense of flow, boundless enthusiasm and a real feeling of discovery at the keyboard. Yet it can be dispiriting to note how quickly this enthusiasm can wane. We feel frustrated over nasty corners in pieces, or simply begin to lose our desire to work on music that is no longer a novelty to our fingers.

How can we maintain our focus and nurture our motivation day in and day out? How can we maintain optimum concentration and positivity over a long period of time without losing the love we initially felt for the repertoire we have chosen to study?

We noted in the previous chapter that long-term plans and methodologies are vital. In the short term, we also need to plan and organise in a 'left-brain' manner. This means setting yourself challenging but realistic targets to strengthen your willpower and motivation. Try using a calendar to write down what you expect to achieve by certain dates in the near future – ideally a week ahead. For example, if you have to learn all of the first movement of Beethoven's F minor Sonata, Op.2 No.1, give yourself until Tuesday evening to learn the exposition, hands separately. You could then continue to map out the rest of the movement by jotting down similar targets for the development section on Thursday, then the recapitulation (still separate hands) on the Saturday.

The following week could be spent gradually getting the piece together. Maybe you could become more specific in your instructions, suggesting things such as 'hands together but with big pauses at the ends of each bar and at a slow tempo up to the end of the development only'. One should never worry if goals such as these are not met – it is all part and parcel of the delightful unpredictability of tactical practising! Simply score out your diary plans and regroup accordingly!

You can be as detailed as you feel necessary when planning in the short term. Map out each practice session so that you have five minute periods of study if you feel that will help keep you focused. It can be revealing to see if pianists are capable of deciding in advance what needs to be done specifically in a practice session; too often inexperienced players are very vague about what they want to achieve, let alone how to go about achieving it!

As well as mapping out practice in advance, motivation and purpose can be helped enormously if you review what happened afterwards. How did your practice hour go this evening at the piano? By the time you'd finished, what had improved? Did you go into repetitive mode and stop thinking? It can be useful to record your practising and listen back analytically. How focused were you on the task in hand? Above all else, were you consistently passionate about the notes you were playing? If you lose your enthusiasm for the music you are trying so hard to master, then there is little point in continuing to practise.

We can reignite our passion for practising repertoire by listening to recordings of great artists playing the same notes. We can read around the repertoire too, and practise mentally. These possibilities have been discussed earlier: to stay motivated and 'on message' requires just as much focus away from the piano as beside it. By that I mean that the extra-pianistic stimuli need to be fully embraced and loved with real commitment. The world is only as big as our imagination allows it to be, so utilise all of your senses to empower your interpretation of Debussy, not only with a sense of orchestration, but also with a love of colours, imagery, smells and taste. Always take the time to reflect, review and consider what you are accomplishing.

Breaks

We can all get tired when practising, and it is only natural that our brains will begin to wander after a certain time, particularly if the room you are playing in has limited ventilation. It is important to take regular breaks and ensure that your blood sugar level is stable. Drink plenty of water, get fresh air and make sure you have lots of sleep every night. Don't sit glued to the piano stool simply because the clock has not exactly reached a certain hour – if you need some time out in order to refocus, take it! There is an absurd culture amongst certain students that unless you work for X number of minutes in a practice slot then you have 'failed' and are being lazy.

Don't practise what does not need to be practised. If your memory and technique are secure, then do not ridicule all of your hard work by deliberately checking if you forget a passage or split notes in it. This scenario is much more common than may be realised, and is particularly harmful when done immediately before a performance.

If you view the practice room as a laboratory in which you can try out various musical 'experiments' with your voicing, colours, the structuring of phrases and so on, then you will never become bored. Music making is all about sound, shape and imagination. The possibilities are indeed infinite and it should never be assumed that the last word has ever been achieved in even the most modest of compositions by an advanced player.

In summary, keep your thoughts focused on the sounds you are producing at each and every moment of your practice time, and view time spent at the instrument preparing repertoire as special, magical moments in your life. As Claudio Arrau once remarked 'I think it is beautiful to practise'. Let's try and ensure that this is always the case.

Time for role play: are you a Wolfgang or a Ludwig?

There has certainly been a tremendous amount written over the years about practising the piano. Text books, magazine articles, websites and blogs consistently stress the importance of organisation, balance, control and calmness. This is all sensible and healthy. The last thing pianists need in their lives is stress! So far, this chapter has followed the orthodox 'calmly organised' approach to practising. We could label this advice as being 'left brained', though we would be wrong to think of it as exclusively intellectual and dull.[44] On the contrary, if developed and nurtured to its full potential then the left-brain aesthetic can evolve into an almost Mozartian approach to music making. If you feel disorganised and want to embrace balance, ease and organisation on a daily basis, then why not try a little role playing, casting yourself as Wolfgang Amadeus?!

A 'Mozartian' approach

Taking a Mozartian approach to music making (and life) means sailing through all challenges with apparently effortless elegance. The absence of noticeable grinding struggle and intense physical effort is all part of a presentational approach – a 'cool dude' style that hides the slogging effort that may very well go into the work. That is not to say that the message delivered needs to be cold or uncommitted. Far from it! The point is that the onlooker is unaware of the sweat that may or may not go into achieving the result. Does a Mozartian struggle? Is there angst and gnashing of teeth? Nobody knows

44 See Chapter 5.

for sure. This makes the Mozartian intriguing, adding a sense of mystery to a style that is already attractive through aesthetic elegance. Indeed, physical actions are executed by Mozartians in as concentrated, fluid and beautifully appealing a manner as possible. In terms of delivery, Mozartians are expert time managers. They dislike wasting energy and effort through mindless practice or unnecessary repetition. Their lifestyles, time management skills and social interactions with the world are all in perfect balance and harmony. They achieve a great deal within the time compartments they allow into their life for their commitments, projects and interests. Concentrated effort means that once something is spoken, written or practised, there is no point in shouting it out loudly again and again. Because Mozartians are so focused, it is possible for them to switch off and appear to forget instantly what they have been working on; they can press a proverbial 'on' button before beginning to work, then press the 'off' button when wishing to stop. Violent outbursts of frustration or angst-ridden sighs of despair have no place in this approach to life. The point is that all that matters is to focus with intense endeavour on the task in hand. This leaves no time for stress and angst. If the task is to practise in moderation each day, then so be it: no procrastination is allowed before getting started, and no post mortems are permitted either afterwards. 'Having done all, stand fast' is the guiding principle. A Mozartian will think before he leaps. Much time will be spent pre-planning, processing and ordering thoughts. When ready to move into action, physical acts (e.g. practising, writing down music, prose etc.) will be dispatched at an extremely fast pace.

To the onlooker, it may well seem as though the Mozartian is rather cold-hearted, even detached. But with the greatest Mozartians nothing could be further from the truth. Their single-minded vision for whatever they decide needs to be done is in fact the consequence of an intensely focused passion for living each and every task 'in the now'.

A 'Beethovenian' approach

On the other hand, you may feel that your practising career has lacked sufficient passion to date, in which case a completely different character is needed for emulation: Ludwig van Beethoven. Those with a Beethovenian approach to music making view practising, like life itself, as an heroic struggle. Special projects are highlighted in turn for all-encompassing, obsessional work with singular focus. This gives glorious meaning to humanity's existence on earth, making Beethovenians feel all the more vibrant, passionate and intense – qualities that they allow all and sundry to witness.

Beethovenians make instinctive, impulsive choices and think later about consequences. They go about life in a flurry of excitement and activity. Their backs are normally proverbially against the wall. When a project is in full flow, time does not seem to exist, but if there is a fixed deadline imposed by others on the completion of a particular task, then time becomes the enemy.

People of this persuasion tend to be red-blooded, intense and fully energised; they can appear frighteningly focused when engaged in whatever it is they are currently passionate about. At other times, they can seem lethargic, unfocused, lacking in concentration, willpower and wherewithal. The daily mundanities of life are neglected, so that 'firefighting' from one crisis to the next tends to be the norm.

Taking a Beethovenian approach means giving your practice sessions all you have got – heart, body and soul – with total abandon. Obsessive, endless repetitions will be the norm as you heroically strive for perfection with full physical, mental and spiritual intensity. If you manage to play with passionate wholeheartedness at full throttle then you will unquestionably succeed in being 'in the zone'. Indeed, this appears to be the only place where Beethovenians seem capable of accomplishing anything they consider worth doing! And when you are 'on fire' in this manner tiredness will never be an issue.

Of course, there is a dramatic flip side to all of this. Life as Beethoven is a rollercoaster ride! If you get into this particular mind-set, once you finish your project there may well be a total collapse. You could find that you are literally incapable of doing anything at all for a few days, even weeks at a time. This is only to be expected; there will always be hubris and nemesis in the lives of people who care intensely and passionately to the point of obsession over individual activities at any given time.

Common sense decrees that the Mozartian model outlined above is the healthiest one to use as a default for regular practising. To role-play in practice as Beethoven is to wear your heart on your sleeve. To do so consistently would be dangerous. Certainly, the approach seems to be diametrically opposed to the advice of all the text books and commentators one can readily think of! Having said that, it is often extremely important to grasp passionate portals of opportunity as soon as they appear! There will always be something mysterious and magical about art, and if a certain piece in the practice studio makes you passionately engaged to the point of near obsession, it would be foolhardy to be checking your watch in order to ensure that you still have time left to practise your Czerny studies. Sometimes it is important to put the rest of your life on hold in pursuit of a singular proverbial holy grail and 'go with the flow'.[45] Chaos, turmoil, stress and extremes can add tremendous colour and intensity to your life if you allow them to. But be warned: a little bit of Beethoven goes a very long way!

---

45 After all, if Handel had not done this for three weeks in 1741 the world may very well have lost *The Messiah*! Reputedly composition of the 'Hallelujah chorus' took only three days to complete. Handel evidently said 'heaven opened' whilst he composed it.

When practice makes imperfect

> 'I was born very, very lazy and I don't always practise very long. But I must say, in my defence, that it is not so good, in a musical way, to over-practise. When you do, the music seems to come out of your pocket. If you play with a feeling of 'Oh, I know this,' you play without that little drop of fresh blood that is necessary – and the audience feels it.'
>
> *Arthur Rubinstein*

'Practice makes perfect', or so popular culture would have us believe. Certainly as pianists we are conditioned from the very first stages to understand that regular, ideally daily, repetitive work at the instrument as prescribed by our teachers will re-enforce and stabilise the notes that we play, producing secure, successful performances. And it works! If you think clearly about objectives and practise with concentrated discipline and focus, then intelligent repetition is a sure-fire way of building control and authority as a player.

But there are many dangers that can block, corrupt and interfere with this process at all levels. From a psychological perspective, insecurity is one of the main causes of negative practising. In this context, the words of the late Sydney Harrison are very perceptive: 'The purpose of practice is to avoid the need to practise!' I couldn't agree more, though it has to be said that a pianist's job is never finished, and that the true artist will never be satisfied. There will always be a need to return and return again to a particular phrase as refinement and shaping continues apace.

What is vital is that a definite separation is understood between practising that has an artistic purpose, and practising which loses intellectual and musical purpose. If a pianist is feeling nervous then it is wrong to assume that a hundred repetitions of the same phrase will lead to confidence and control. In fact, the repetitions can lead to more nerves! This is because practising reinforces what you are doing – if you are tense and uncertain on the first two repetitions of a phrase, then no number of additional 'play-throughs' will help. What is vital is the ability to analyse and understand problems. Let's look at the closing A minor arpeggios in Beethoven's ubiquitous bagatelle *Für Elise*.

Many younger players find this passage challenging, as the position shifts can be unreliable, with split notes and unwanted accents appearing instead of effortless control and grace. Begin with silent shadowing of the keys: play the right hand 'silently' to check fingering. Continue by working on the actual position shifts themselves, making sure that you are aware how your hands and wrists move. Try 'blind practice' and holding the first note of every three for a little longer. By all means review what you have done by playing through the passage at the end of your practice session, but do not play it more than once. If it is successful, fine, if not, then review what you are doing and work again. The point is that practising has to be different from playing. And once you have achieved what you set out to do, stop!

Like Rubinstein ... from planet Pluto!

Piano teachers the world over all know how frustrating it can be to teach a talented student who, for whatever reason, has not been practising. Quite often the reasons for a lack of preparation can be perfectly legitimate. A student I taught in 2015–16 was a very talented and enthusiastic musician, but because he was under extreme academic pressure there had not been a lot of piano work in the run up to A level exams. Despite this, we continued working as conscientiously as possible in each lesson, tackling fingering, discussing ways to practise, listening to other recordings, using my own playing as a kind of 'roadmap' for possibilities, and even practising in the lessons too! But sadly, all of these scenarios eventually passed their proverbial sell-by-date. Conventional pedagogy seemed over-spent. We had exhausted discussion, practice tips, general overviews and even supervised practice. What to do? There was nothing left but to hear the whole of César Franck's mighty fugue (from his *Prelude, Chorale and Fugue*) and see the current state of play ...

... so, the first ten minutes of the lesson proceeded with what was unquestionably a faltering and insecure rendering of that fugue. But because the student had lots of ideas and good intentions for every phrase of the piece, there seemed to be hope and inspiration in what he was playing – albeit from a distorted, incoherent perspective. Suddenly an idea emerged in my head that proved to be a lifeline for the remainder of the lesson. I warmed to the task: 'Actually your performance is a great one – as great as Rubinstein's or Richter's! It's just that it is as though you are performing from a distant planet. I want you to imagine that you are performing to me from planet Pluto! I am receiving your great performance only sporadically and in small chunks, because the observatory from which I receive your sounds (coming many millions of miles away in outer space) can only hear a couple of bars at a time – sometimes it can only capture five or six notes of your performance in one go before there is a gap in proceedings! Give me your great performance again, but this time in micro-chunks. Imagine you are performing from the distant planet Pluto, and before each chunk, there is inevitably a long delay. Use that time to 'pre-play' in your mind what you are about to do, then go ahead and play it up to tempo, with the exact voicing, shape and characterisation that ideally you would like. If the result of your playing is not immediately perfect, then imagine astronomers down on planet Earth are at fault! Their receivers are not up to the task so you will have to proceed by replaying the fragment again and again if necessary! Keep repeating it until you are absolutely convinced by what you hear.

And so, the work began! We had lift-off! It immediately became apparent that inspiration was in the air. At times the student only played a five-note passage and, even though passages as small as this needed several repetitions, the quality of what was being produced had beauty, artistic energy and focus. The lesson ended up lasting for well over the scheduled hour, but by the end the whole fugue had been covered, and every note of it was produced with authoritative, beautiful sounds and at appropriate tempos. What could have been a frustrating lesson spent hearing vague and approximate attempts was transformed into a really focused session in which no compromises were made in terms of the quality of playing. The lesson closed with a short discussion about the teaching methods of the great 19th century pedagogue Theodore Leschetizky.[46] He always emphasised the need for pupils to work in tiny segments of music at a time, fine tuning, polishing and honing in on each part of a work separately. By bringing loving and intense care to micro-chunks of music, seeds are sewn that will grow into glorious trees and eventually forests of beautiful music.

46   See *Piano Technique in Practice*, 164–67.

11 The benefits of injury

Accidents or injuries leading to enforced layoffs are a musician's nightmare. To a fired-up performer with a burning desire to practise and perform there is surely nothing more wasteful than a broken wrist or an inflamed tendon. Depression, frustration, anger and bitterness would seem natural human reactions to physical limitations that apparently curtail all musical activities, at least in the short term. What could be more negative than injury?

Perhaps a lot! The truth is that it is our own attitudes that determine whether or not something is positive or negative. If pianists find themselves in positions whereby practising is impossible in the short term, then there is still much that they can do to improve musicianship, artistry and pianism. I would go as far as to say that there is nothing that cannot be practised away from the instrument![47] Provided the injury is not a permanent one, and playing will return in the relatively near future, then any layoff can and indeed should be experienced positively. Let's look at some of the 'practising' that could be developed on a regular and intense basis by musicians who find themselves injured and therefore unable to practise conventionally.

Memory

Over the years, I have met several short-sighted pianists who needed to memorise their repertoire because the practicalities of fitting enlarged music scores onto piano stands proved too difficult to overcome. Though on the face of it these determined individuals faced enormous challenges, in the long term there is no question that their musicianship benefitted considerably from the efforts of 'pre-hearing' their repertoire internally. The great pianist Walter Gieseking was trained to do precisely this by his mentor Karl Leimer, and his case is frequently cited as an inspiration. Could it be that his precocious memory skills and unparalleled ear for colour and voicing in Debussy were at least partly developed via the pre-play memory technique that he was taught? I like to think so. Certainly, we have already seen in Chapter 7 that the internalisation of music is crucial for a sense of confidence, security and conviction in performance. There is nothing worse than relying on external apparatus as a prop for 'success'. If you can play through entire movements of Beethoven sonatas in your head without the need to move your fingers around, then you have great inner strength.

---

47   See Chapter 7 for more on 'pianoless' practising.

Background research

Injury layoffs are excellent times to increase curiosity, awareness and understanding of music in its broadest cultural context. Though many younger pianists in particular gravitate to the instrument mainly because they enjoy the physical thrill of keyboard contact, this is but one dimension of the total piano playing experience.

When an injury prevents you from practising then you will have time to expand on 'pianoless' practice to a huge extent. Do not restrict yourself to just piano music – a newly acquired love of the six Op.18 string quartets and first two symphonies of Beethoven will transform any interpretation of the *Pathetique* sonata. Approaches to colour, bowing and structure that are adopted by the Roger Norringtons, Simon Rattles, Tokyo or Takás Quartets are just as worth 'emulating' as the latest high powered flourish from Lang Lang or Yuja Wang!

Not that imitation is the reason for listening to performances from others, least of all other pianists. The whole subject of when to 'study' commercial recordings is a long and complex one, simply because pianists need to learn to stand on their own artistic feet carefully and gradually. But with injury, this ceases to be an issue – enforced piano layoffs are a golden opportunity to broaden your cultural horizons through long listening sessions. When you are fully healthy there simply isn't the time to do as much of this invaluable work as would be ideal. And don't limit yourself to 'passive' study – use the extra hours to try transcriptions of your repertoire for other combinations of instruments. Try improvising or writing sets of variations from favourite motifs in your set pieces. The sky really is the limit.

The inner conception: recovery from all setbacks

We can be injured mentally and spiritually too. There is no question that self-esteem and confidence are unequivocally connected to physical, mental and spiritual health and wellbeing. Ultimately, inspiration from studying music away from the piano is of vital importance for all kinds of setbacks. If you have a less-than-successful piano lesson, or a disappointing experience in a public competition or examination, it is reinvigorating to use mental practising as a means of wiping the slate clean via visualisation.

Use 'pianoless' practising as a general 'negativity buster' to help us whenever anything negative in life affects our ability to focus and concentrate solely on our music at the piano.

To create a strong, internalised vision not only of how you want to play, but of how you want to feel as you play is a powerful skill, and one that we should all devote considerable time to developing and maintaining. Experience has shown that visualisation is the same as any other aspect of piano technique: if you don't use it, you lose it! Sharpen and maintain your mental practice on a daily basis as a means of strengthening your spirit.

By nourishing your music making via internalised practice, by empowering your inner conceptions, you are 'healing' yourself and reaching a source of strength that no army of physiotherapists or even psychiatrists and counsellors ever can. As has already been mentioned in Chapter 7, visualisation should extend towards the engagement of all of your senses away from the instrument. In this way, we can truly heal ourselves inwardly and so rise above 'Dis Ease', emerging much stronger than ever before.

So, whilst one would never wish for a pianist to experience physical or psychological discomfort to the extent that a break from playing is enforced, we can close this brief but important discussion by asserting that there is no need to view injury in any way other than a positive means for artistic development. We learn from all our experiences in life, and when you return to playing not only will you be 'healed', but you will have a far greater sense of mental, spiritual and creative purpose, strength and discipline.

12 Anxiety and stage-fright

The unknown factor

The late Gina Bachauer once said that no matter how prepared you are for a concert, you never really know what will happen during the performance itself. This mysterious lack of certainty adds lots of thrills and excitement to the performance experience, but the flipside can be overwhelmingly negative, leading in some sad instances to performers losing all physical control, being unable to even remember the first note of a piece, or in extreme instances, being unable to set foot on the stage at all. Concert nerves can affect amateur, student and professional musicians alike, often coming in phases or cycles in playing careers. Clearly everyone who plays to others needs, on occasion, to harness concert anxiety. This applies as much to those preparing for their Carnegie recital hall debuts as to those who only wish to perform small bagatelles in front of friends.

Rituals and routines

Minimise the negative sides of the unknown elements associated with performing by enjoying a calmly ordered sense of routine immediately before preparing to play. It is vital to organise the day of your performance as precisely as you can, with a very firm timetable over trivial day to day things such as transport arrangements, rehearsal times and so on. Organisation most certainly makes the 'unknown factor' much easier to handle. Many performers find it extremely helpful to sleep in the afternoon before a concert. You may object that you would be too emotionally fraught to do this, but the ability to 'cat nap' can be practised and mastered, and artists of the calibre of Alfred Brendel and Claudio Arrau reputedly found sleep to be of enormous help in preparing successfully for the artistic challenges ahead.

You can spend the final hours before your stage entrance practising visualisation as suggested in Chapter 7. Indeed, positive visualisation of happiness and comfort on stage has to be practised and nurtured on a daily basis in the weeks and months leading up to a performance. But on the concert day itself, meditation is arguably the most important aspect of practising. You may find it helpful to try the following meditative exercise whilst lying down on the green room floor. It is something I have practised regularly for over three decades immediately before countless concerts and owes much to 'alphanetics', a particular form of transcendental meditation my father kindly introduced me to back in the 1980s.[48]

48 See www.alphanetics.org for further information on the 'life dynamics fellowship course', originally 14 audio tapes aimed at the subconscious mind and relaxing you to the 'alpha' level where your brain vibrates between 14 and 7 cycles per second.

Meditation in the green room

1 Lie down on the floor in the Alexander position with your head propped-up with a book.

2 Start breathing slowly and deeply with your eyes shut.

3 Focus mentally on each part of your body in turn. Relax everything as you do a mental 'tour' of your whole being. Work upwards from your toes to the top of your head, including your eyes.

4 Begin counting down calmly from eight to zero, continuing to relax, taking deep breaths and keeping your eyes closed.

Level eight Aim for total physical relaxation. Enjoy the moment, wait, then when this feels effortless, glide towards level seven.

Level seven Slow down your thought processes, enjoy.

Level six Thoughts are now taken at a *molto largo* pulse. Linger there, then count to level five.

Level five Feel physically lighter; your body gently lifts upwards as you float beautifully and calmly.

Level four Sunshine, warmth and an inner glow fills your entire being with a deep pleasurable contentment. Take time to savour this.

Level three There should be absolutely no thoughts other than 'of the moment'. Live in the present completely.

Level two You are virtually asleep. Give in to it; let go.

Level one This is your most creative state, poised as it is on the cusp of sleep. Take a deep breath, relax and maintain complete tranquillity and calm. You can then imagine whatever positive ambition(s) you have in front of you on your big 'cinema screen'. The possibilities should include nerve-free performances, with enjoyment of each and every moment of the piece in question, and most certainly no 'end-gaining' angst whatsoever.

After level one's 'film' has run its course, slowly count back from one up to eight. Then, slowly, but with calm, confident energy, stand up.

Nerves and terror

Nerves have an image problem. All too often they are regarded as totally negative, destructive and powerful. In addition to their reputation for completely wrecking a perfectly secure and well-prepared interpretation in a live concert, nerves are also given the credit by some of having totally destroyed all enjoyment permanently and irrevocably for performing. Sadly, it is common to meet enthusiastic players who refuse to play even a simple C major scale in your presence, claiming that the mere thought of being heard by even one solitary human being leaves them feeling threatened, nauseous and totally out of control.

But just a moment – why do so many of us watch horror films, go back time and time again for rollercoaster rides and take up risky sports such as bungee jumping? Are we not told regularly by the media that a little stress is good for you; that we can take pleasure from living 'life on the edge', at least from time to time? The very nature of excitement always involves a little risk, and our day to day existence would be dreadfully dull without this element of danger. Nerves are an essential part of 'thrilling excitement', so it is not desirable to airbrush them out of our lives. Rather let us, in the words of Ronald Stevenson, 'tune nerves to concert pitch' and find ways in which heightened, energised alertness can bring added pleasure to our playing.

We are all human, and this means we can feel out of control when we are in new, unfamiliar or difficult situations. When our instinctive antennae pick up stress our biological reactions, directly inherited from Neanderthal man, urge us to take flight. We begin to perspire, hyperventilate, shake and tremble. When in 'Neanderthal mode', pianists commonly start to rush manically, crashing and thrashing ever onwards, but never upwards. In these situations, all preparation is forgotten and the 'interpretation' (if it can be called that) is simply an effort to survive through to the final note. Learning to cope with rushing (arguably one of the most frightening forms of nervous anxiety) begins with a focus on living in the 'now'. Avoid at all costs what followers of the Alexander Technique refer to as 'end gaining' – the inability to concentrate on what you are doing at any one given moment because of anxieties over what will happen later. Savouring each moment in performance is a sure-fire way of overcoming terror. In your daily practice at the instrument the most vital thing on which to concentrate is firm rhythmic anchorage.

Anti-rush exercises

There are many ways in which busy passages can be practised so that a firm sense of rhythmic anchorage will always be maintained in performance. I strongly recommend the following exercises for all troublesome passages:

1 Play the passage with each hand separately whilst using your non-playing hand to tap out the pulse on the lid of the piano. For some reason, this seems more effective than simply tapping out the pulse with one or both feet, but of course foot tapping is certainly also an option.

2 Add in off-beat accents. So often it is the weak beats, or the weak parts of beats, that are skimmed over in problematic passages. By consciously giving these a rhythmic 'kick' in practice, you are feeding an awareness of them into your subconscious and so nurturing their significance into the passage in question.

3 Conduct with one hand whilst practising the other. This is particularly useful when dealing with accompaniment figurations over filigree passagework, as

is frequently encountered in the works of Chopin. Conducting with natural ease and a sense of direction will encourage you to feel the shape of the phrases you play. It is also useful to sing the melodic line whilst conducting as this will encourage a sense of the music's pulse from within.

4 Walk, dance and skip! Rushing is essentially an inability to control and harness a sense of the music's innate rhythm. Therefore, it is very helpful to move physically in time to your repertoire. Record your performances, then try to walk in time to them. Can you feel a watertight sense of pulse? Does your playing make you want to tap your toes or even dance as you listen back to it? If you are unhappy with what you hear from a rhythmic perspective, begin again. Try to hear the music in your inner ear, and dance along in silence. If you can conceive a perfect rhythm in abstract, it will be much easier to attempt to recreate this 'aural photograph' when you resume practising.

5 Take time to explore hidden motifs, and learn appoggiaturas and suspensions. Find subsidiary voices and figurations and make sure that you can always hear them when you play. This is an excellent and artistically stimulating means of controlling the pulse when you feel nervous.

6 I recommend that baroque pieces are always practised with several different approaches to articulation. By mixing *staccato* and *legato* in various permutations it is possible to feel more in control of the pulse. This leads to an increased sense of musical awareness when it finally comes to public performance.

7 Take a small section of the music and count out loud in demisemiquavers as you play. When you can do this, take the same passage but count out the semiquavers as you practise, then take the quavers, crotchets, minims and even the whole bars in turn. This procedure is similar to looking through binoculars at the same object but from different perspectives. It is particularly useful in slow movements of classical sonatas, but can be effective in any passage where a lack of rhythmic control is evident.

Fear of forgetting

Another common worry that performers usually cite as a reason for stage-fright is memory. This has already been discussed in *Piano Technique in Practice* but needs reconsideration here as it is a major source of anxiety for many players.[49] A fear of forgetting notes prior to performance involuntarily manifests negative visualisation, making memory lapses more likely to occur. In performance a single memory lapse tends to stimulate another, and can lead to post-performance trauma in which the mental re-enactment of the forgotten passages stimulates fear for the future. How then to break this vicious cycle?

49 *Piano Technique in Practice*, Chapter 18, 168–75.

Firstly, we should all realise that music is about sounds, not circus tricks – it does not matter if you intend to use the score or not in performance, it is the quality of your interpretation that matters. Regardless of the whether or not you perform from memory you should be able to play your repertoire in private without reference to the printed page. This is simply because the ability to internalise your repertoire makes ownership and understanding of it more likely than if you need to stare constantly at the notes. I would go as far as to say fool-proof internalised memory generates so much belief and confidence that it can completely evaporate nervous anxiety on the concert stage!

In *Piano Technique in Practice* five basic memory methods were outlined, and each approach needs a relaxed, loving aesthetic if they are to achieve any degree of success.[50] A word of caution: working exclusively from memory without due consideration for the interpretation can lead to more anxiety. The brain needs to focus on the musical substance of your repertoire in order to be fully engaged. The artistic vacuum created by musical disengagement allows nervous anxiety to move in.

Concentration during performance

Even with the ability to harness rhythm and control memory, nerves cannot always be overcome. Many of us have suffered from a lack of self-belief and a tendency to hear nagging voices in our heads as we perform. Sometimes our minds simply wander and think random thoughts. This can be particularly true at the beginning of a performance. I still remember with amusement how, as a 17-year-old, I could not stop thinking bizarre thoughts about kippers and toast when beginning a Bach Prelude and Fugue during my important Royal Academy of Music performers' diploma recital! It was irritating at the time, but there was nothing I could do about it. Distractions of this ilk can be overcome by singing inwardly. Never think ahead; follow the melodic contour and the phrasing as it rises and falls, and you will immediately feel more focused. When the music is more motoric than melodic, as in numerous examples from Bartók's *Mikrokosmos* and pieces by Prokofiev, Ginastera and countless others, it is also important to inwardly dance as you play. Feel the pulse as a live, throbbing energised force emanating from within. Personally, I find it easiest to focus on the sounds being produced in performance by refraining from looking down at my hands as I play. And it goes without saying that phrasing, rhythmic awareness and the avoidance of hand-eye contact are all things that can and should be prepared in the practice studio.

---

50 Namely aural, visual, analytical, kinesthetic and rote memory (*Piano Technique in Practice*, 269–70).

Physical side-effects of nerves

Nerves may affect you badly in a physical way: necks can stiffen, fingers feel like jelly, and lower legs start to shake. Deep, relaxed and natural breathing will work wonders, and is something that should be a regular part of your daily warm-up routine prior to practice. 'Always remember to breathe' was the advice of my piano teacher at school when questioned about overcoming concert anxiety, and indeed a lack of thought for airflow during a concert is a major cause of anxiety and technical insecurity.[51] Diet is another vital factor. All athletes appreciate the importance of knowing when and what to eat prior to performing, so it is surprising how 'hit or miss' dietary considerations tend to be with musicians. You stand a worse chance harnessing concert anxiety if you go on stage with a lack of blood sugar or a bloated feeling caused by eating starchy food immediately beforehand. Diet, particularly the timing of diet, is an art form in itself for all musicians. It is worth finding out what works best for you as an individual. Speaking personally as a performer and teacher, apples are my special nerve-busting superfood! Many of my students do as I tend to do these days and eat nothing but this fruit in the final two hours before a performance. Obviously, it is vital to have energy, yet at the same time it is essential to refrain from the over-eating that leads to a frightening sense of sluggishness in a concert situation. I find that a protein-filled meal five hours before 'curtains up', followed by a steady dose of natural sugar from apples is a winning combination that ensures maximum comfort, confidence and energy, especially if it is combined with at least an hour or two of sleep, a hot bath, some light reading and a pleasant walk in the great outdoors. If you want to conquer nerves, pamper yourself!

Also on the positive side, remember that nerves will always be controllable if you have an excellent technique. Coping with anxiety on stage is all part of being rigorously trained as a pianist, and this brings us to the most important point of all: if your complete preparation is strong, then nerves will never have a negative effect. On the contrary, they will bring an added 'edge' and excitement to your playing. But in order for this to happen, your technique needs to be reliable, the organisation and day to day management of your lifestyle needs to be consistently reviewed, and – above all else – you need to be fully on top of everything you play publicly. You need to rehearse and re-rehearse performing; invite friends and relatives over to your practice room, dress up as you would do for a recital, and perform for them. You should also record and listen back critically to all of your mock recitals, and remember that you will not feel really familiar with a piece in live performance until you have played it several times in concerts.

Preparation takes time – indeed Ferruccio Busoni famously used to refrain from airing a new work in public until he had worked at it and thought it through for at least two years beforehand. If you are fully prepared, and you have done everything possible to secure your interpretation of the repertoire you intend

---

51   See *Piano Technique in Practice*, 27–29.

to perform, then nerves become an important stimulant towards musical expression. They give an element of the 'unknown' to playing and make you look forward with eager anticipation to your next concert, competitive festival or exam. Let's be grateful for at least a little bit of 'controlled terror' in our musical lives. Nerves are there to be celebrated and reappraised as a vibrant positive phenomenon!

Part 4
Dependence or independence?

13 Spoon-feeding

For the teacher, there can be no more noble a goal than to make him/herself dispensable to their students. Creating independence, enabling them to think, work and develop by themselves, is the ultimate pedagogical aim, guiding and mentoring them as they become individual artists in their own right.

But to a large extent, education means learning from the examples of others. Guidance via imitation has a long and noble tradition not only in the teaching of instrumental playing but also in composition and indeed in the other arts too. Italian Renaissance painters in their apprenticeships frequently 'copied' the works of older masters to obtain technical progress, whilst Bach devoted hours of his youth to copying out, note by note, the works of past composers such as Buxtehude and J.C.F. Fischer, amongst many others.

For pianists, learning via imitation means rapidly assimilating lots and lots of instructions, ideas and concepts. Copying the approaches of teachers inevitably involves 'hands on' detailed instruction from them which, over the course of several years, can often take hundreds of hours to impart. Clearly there are grave dangers here, as the blind 'hero worship' of a celebrated mentor can lead star-struck pupils towards too literal a reproduction of one approach to playing.

Let's categorise spoon-feeding into positive and negative. Positive spoon-feeding in pedagogy is an absolute necessity in that it develops students quickly without stifling their ability to think and work for themselves. Negative spoon-feeding is really 'musical cloning', which involves limiting the creative energy of music, and is done without regard for a student's understanding, or lack of understanding. It leads to unoriginality, generic decision-making and artistic boredom.

Negative spoon-feeding: copycats and militant note-by-note teaching

In the recording era, there are pianists who opt literally to copy not only the tempos and broad interpretive choices from commercial discs, but also the most miniscule of details – phrasing, *rubato*, ornamentation, colouring, voicings and choice of pedalling. This literal imitation has been traditionally frowned upon by the musical community. To rely on the decisions of others is to risk stifling your own creativity. It implies a fear of making your own decisions. In practice, imitation often fails to capture the genius of a Rachmaninov or a Horowitz but can be successful in reproducing mannerisms, such as extreme *ritardandi* and *accelerandi*, the splitting of chords, or abrupt changes in tempo.

In the past decade or so the phenomenon that is YouTube has made it even easier for young pianists to imitate the art of others, with facial expressions and body movements commonly being emulated as well as musical qualities. It is especially alarming, and not so uncommon, to find youthful players who cannot read music easily, but persevere by repeatedly listening to tracks of small but impressive pieces (such as Rachmaninov's C sharp minor Prelude or Chopin's E flat Nocturne, Op 9. No.2) until they can copy what they see and hear. Whilst copying is something which no-one should ever practise as a central means towards musical development, it is worth acknowledging that the technique of being a copycat has its (limited) place. Viewed in the spirit of a renaissance apprentice artist, it could encourage a young 21st century pianist to understand the choices of more experienced players, which could prove motivational if they are assimilated into a more enlightened and broader musical picture.

Militant note-by-note teaching

Teachers risk stifling their students if they indulge in too much note-by-note criticism. I have lost count of the number of times I have spoken to colleagues who confess to being unable to play particular works (often pieces by Chopin such as the *Barcarolle*, fourth Ballade or *Berceuse*) simply because they endured a series of traumatic spoon-fed lessons on the work in question from a bullying teacher. We are talking about epic-length piano lessons here in which single chords, notes or even gestures leading up to single notes are stopped and stopped again by the teacher, who more often than not appears in aggressive mode: 'No, no! Do that again! And again!'

What is disturbing about this is not so much the fact that complete lessons can be spent on single phrases but that the endless repetitions are done without real explanation of why they are being done.

Positive spoon-feeding

Clearly there are times when an inexperienced pianist needs to have his/ her hand held for every detail. It could be that the repertoire in question is totally out of the pianist's comfort zone, or that a crisis in confidence makes it impossible for them to cope on their own. Perhaps the piece in question involves new technical challenges, or is hard to memorise. Perhaps time is of the essence and a performance must be in place at short notice.

Whatever the reasons for spoon-feeding, communication and clear explanations from teacher to pupil are essential. A Plato-like, 'question and answer' style of delivery is perfectly compatible with instructions from the tutor that need to be followed and 'imitated' by the student. Above all, positive spoon-feeding necessitates that pianists really listen to what they are doing. Aural awareness should be encouraged alongside a healthy, inspirational need to strive through repetition towards a refined beauty and cultivated artistic vision. Taking joy and delight in gradually moulding the smallest of musical phrases towards an artistic Parnassus should be the ultimate goal, an approach made famous by the great pianist-composer Theodor Leschetizky.

We can emulate the Leschetizky approach today by working in small musical sections during a piano lesson as a shared laboratory experiment between mentor and student. As repetition follows on repetition, both teacher and pupil should be able to delight in a sense of evolution; enjoy the journey towards a shared goal.

Take on board all of the law-giving and spoon-feeding you can, then later, in your own time, assimilate what you have learnt and make it your own (or reject it outright). Having said that, even the most legendary of performers will find it much more interesting to rediscover and reinvent familiar repertoire each time they encounter it. If a masterclass is predicable it is usually because the 'master' is overly fixated with his/her own approach, ignoring the unique circumstances of the student who is playing, and therefore spoon-feeding without musical sensitivity.

In summary, negative spoon-feeding is where there is no understanding. Students fail to comprehend why they are being asked to do something and as a result become more insecure. Their uncertainty leads to more dependency on their mentor which leads to an absence of ownership of their playing. This lack of independence limits their potential for self-development and creativity; the music is either 'right' or 'wrong' and therefore limited, even boing.

Positive spoon-feeding in piano lessons occurs when everything a teacher requests is asked for and delivered with a clear purpose and explanation. The rapidity of delivery, the necessity of repetitions of small musical fragments will always be accompanied by communicative dialogue so that the student understands the principles that make it necessary for him to be drip-fed information.

14 Avoiding dogmatism

In the vast universe of pianists, pedagogues, recordings, traditions and musical egos, it is all too easy for individuals to become overwhelmed. Teachers, editions and critics frequently offer young pianists diametrically opposing opinions about every aspect of music making. Moreover, individuals (most commonly teachers) often contradict themselves from one lesson to the next.[52] Why are things so complex? Who, and what, is right and wrong?! Finding your own way as a pianist, taking ownership of what you do as a musician, has all too frequently been an extremely confusing and elongated process. How to find answers and credos that are true to you, rather than to an overbearing mentor or a strongly marketed new state-of-the-art ürtext edition?[53] And are any of us really sure of what our true musical selves are anyway? As musicians, and indeed as humans, we are a complex synthesis of all kinds of conscious, subconscious and superconscious influences, so trying to forge a pathway forward that 'pleases' us and the world without losing sincerity may, on one level, appear impossible to accomplish.

But really there is no need to bother about all of that one bit! Rather than worry, let's identify approaches for dealing with the whole business of individuality and independence. Therein lies something of a vacuum in piano teaching so far. By considering issues one by one, by suggesting approaches and techniques to establish and maintain healthy relationships with piano gurus, editions, past and present performances, the ego and our inbuilt need as humans for approval, we can survive! We can find a way to progress on a daily basis without seeking an unhealthy need for approval from the world, which is a totally different thing from finding empathy with others via music making. Hopefully we can also come to the realisation that there is no contradiction whatsoever between taking on board all kinds of influences and maintaining artistic individuality.

It is only human nature to look for definitive truths in life. Many of us have a deep-seated need to find classification and order, to decide that something is 'right' whilst something else is 'wrong'. Neatly packaging our lives into boxes gives a sense of control that can possibly be considered reassuring. However, art is not as simple as that. In piano playing this can immediately be seen in the recording catalogue, in many of the impressive, memorable, controversial and celebrated versions of Bach's *Well-Tempered Clavier* that have appeared over the decades. Start by comparing Edwin Fischer's breathtakingly beautiful version of this seminal work from the 1930s with András Schiff's landmark

---

52 This was reputedly true of Artur Schnabel who, when questioned on this subject, apparently asked 'Am I not allowed to change my mind?!'
53 Indeed even the authority of ürtext editions can be hotly contested: I'm indebted to Douglas Finch for recently recalling Rosalyn Tureck's question 'How ür is the ür of your ürtext?' during a masterclass at the University of Western Ontario.

issue for Decca from the 1980s. Both are authoritative and inspirational, but also as radically dissimilar as it is possible to be! Add into the mix equally diverse, individual and striking recordings from Sviatoslav Richter, Angela Hewitt, Bernard Roberts, Glenn Gould and Daniel Barenboim and it quickly becomes self-evident that any music lover intent on choosing a 'winning recording' is severely limiting their musical values and experiences. Ranking these performances in order of preference is a game young, musically inexperienced children could enjoy playing; mature listeners may find greater fulfilment if they can admire and even love more than one extremely contrasted interpretive approach of a great masterpiece!

This may take time to develop, but it is worth cultivating. Aspiring pianists need to be open-minded, flexible and willing to experiment if they are to develop into authoritative players.

I strongly believe that the democratisation of your inner musical values will unquestionably lead to playing that is less predictable and more flexible! This is because subjective opinions and whimsical spur-of-the-moment decisions all have their place in creative piano playing. It is so much more fulfilling and stimulating to practise with your creative antennae constantly turned on to fresh suggestions, no matter how wayward these ideas may first appear. We should also celebrate the fact that as individuals ourselves we can constantly change our own minds. Whilst integrity and sincerity are vital qualities, avoiding dogmatism and remaining inspired by alternative approaches will keep us artistically young. It is all part and parcel of remaining curiously creative and energised at the piano for many decades to come.

There are certain things that can always be labelled as 'wrong'. If you play the (*pianissimo*) opening of Beethoven's C major 'Waldstein' sonata, Op.53 at *fortissimo*, then that is arguably a greater crime than playing it *pianissimo* in D flat major! Ürtext editions provide us with a sense of authenticity as we prepare our interpretations of the great works in the piano literature. In this sense, we must see ourselves as curators of musical museums, with a responsibility for presenting to listeners the glory and integrity of every note. Certainly, we live in an era where there is more information at our fingertips than ever before. We have sources and performances on tap for study that should lead us towards authority and integrity with regard to textual fidelity.

Techniques for coping with contradictions

How do musicians cope with contrasted views? Do too many cooks spoil the proverbial broth?! If you play the same piece to several different but equally renowned teachers, you should not expect to receive similar advice. And you should not expect any one teacher to be more 'correct' in their approach than the others! There are as many different ways of approaching interpretation as there are pianists. In music, it is not so much whether you are 'correct' or 'wrong' that counts as how you are correct or wrong. No self-respecting teacher will criticise an interpretive choice from a student if that particular choice works. But if phrasing, tempo, tone quality or any other element in a pianist's playing lacks conviction, then questions will inevitably be raised. Quite often these questions may appear to be inconsistent; so many times one hears of students becoming angry because one week their teacher will tell them to play one way, only to suggest something very different the following week! Contradictions and U-turns are all part and parcel of piano teaching, but this can be one of the hardest issues for students to come to terms with.

Begin by seeing contradictions as a positive phenomenon. Differences of viewpoint add to the rich tapestry of life and are one of the joyful things that make music so vibrant. Thank goodness we are all so different! If you are fortunate enough to experience the vivid contrast that comes from playing a single piece to three or four different pianist-teachers in the same week, on a piano camp for example, then make sure you take time to celebrate the ideological, technical and musical conflicts that will inevitably arise. But prepare yourself emotionally – you will need to be strong enough not to get confused or discouraged. It is all too easy for students to become tense and nervous before playing to new teachers. In order to gain the most from one-off sessions with different pianists, you must relax and concentrate on being as receptive as possible. You are there to soak up new ideas and concepts and find inspiration that would otherwise not be available.

Firstly, I recommend turning up to each session with a different copy of the music. You can then compare and contrast the different fingerings, markings and suggestions without seeing scribbled out marks from one teacher attempting to superimpose his or her fingering over another's! I also recommend recording the lessons (but always ask permission first). Give yourself a little breathing space to take notes afterwards. Most importantly of all, relax and focus on being receptive before a lesson begins. Wipe the proverbial slate clean and start afresh as though you have never had a lesson on the piece from anyone else before. Don't worry about losing your identity – in this instance it is often a good policy to let the teacher lead the way. Do what he says, even if you disagree profoundly with what is being offered. As lesson times are precious, they are usually best spent in a receptive, positive and non-argumentative mode. If there is an audience present, it is worth bearing in mind that they are there to receive inspiration and enlightenment from the approach of the master-teacher. Sadly, this can lead to abuse and exploitation from the celebrity figure. Famous musicians who use the masterclass scenario as a means of asserting their power and authority are beneath contempt. But equally, students who turn up to perform in masterclasses solely to show how 'brilliant' they are also deserve little respect.

In a more general sense, piano lessons fall into one of three distinct classifications (all of them equally valid). Firstly, we have a traditional 'masterclass' format as described above, in which the great teacher dictates everything. Let's call this a 'totalitarian' approach. The second category involves lots of questions and is 'platonic', with the student taking the lead. Free marketers who believe that in education the student is the consumer and the teacher the service provider expect this approach. 'Free marketising' in the piano studio takes longer than totalitarianism, but the results are nearly always inspiring for the pupil, who will feel ownership of the music. There will be a feel-good factor for the student at the end of lessons; a sense that the capitalist economy truly is working brilliantly well and that the teacher is catering for individual needs.

The third type of teaching is much more subtle and involves a combined partnership in which teacher and student unite and strive towards the common purpose of musical inspiration. It is unquestionably the most spiritual, selfless approach. There will always be an unpredictable element and much will depend on how the teacher and pupil relate to each other. Perhaps this style of teaching is rarer in one-off lessons as the mentor and the student get to know each other over an extended period of time. This could be labelled 'reaction teaching', with both teacher and student responding to the immediacy of the music making in instinctive, musically sensitive ways. Personally, I believe that though all three approaches to pedagogy are essential for pianists to experience, option three affords the greatest likelihood of transcending worldly concerns, of reaching 'the zone', of finding inspiration and true creativity. At its very best it provides pupil and mentor with a loss of self-consciousness, of egotistical concerns and nervousness. This creative state is an ideal. The odds of achieving it are enhanced when both student and teacher are relaxed, open to new suggestions and deeply in love with the music that is being studied.

Let's now look at these contrasted pedagogical approaches in practice. Interpretations of the works of J.S. Bach are always going to be viewed in highly subjective terms. The celebrated C major Prelude from Book One of the *Well-Tempered Clavier* can be played in strict tempo with no pedal, limited overlapping between notes and only a few, restricted dynamics.

A totalitarian teacher could well insist on this as an ideological necessity – Bach cannot be played with pedal! Alternatively, it could be played with lashings of *sostenuto* pedal, extreme dynamics and *rubato*. Free marketers could coax out a student's inner desires by using Platoesque questions as a means of identifying personal 'choices' and preferences from the fee-paying client's own motivations.

However, there are many other possibilities away from these two extremes. Glenn Gould's stance in his recording uses a mixture of slurred and *staccato* notes in each bar to create an almost playfully mannered *scherzando* variation

of what people expect to hear! Perhaps a spiritually enlightened virtuoso
piano teacher would begin a lesson on this piece by playing some recordings
of Yo Yo Ma, Pablo Casals and Paul Tortelier in the Bach unaccompanied 'cello
suites. The lesson could then move on to improvisation, with the students
extemporising around the chord sequence of the Prelude, then seeing where
this led in terms of pedal, non-pedal, *rubato* and dynamics.

Let's move onto Mozart and the closing section of the second movement in his
A major Piano concerto K488.

The notes on the printed page are skeletal, and opinion in past generations
was divided over whether performers should stick exclusively to the spartan
text, or add decorations around it (i.e. using the printed notes as pitch points
from which individual creativity can flow). Even if pianists largely agree on the
latter option in the 21st century (not all do by any means!) there are those who
consistently stick to the same decorations for every single performance, and
those who prefer to improvise and leave details to the whim of the moment
(option three teachers). In addition, within each of these approaches there are
so many other possibilities for free marketers to utilise. Should the pianist use
pedal? Should the dynamic level remain *sotto voce*, or is a sonorous, operatic
stance appropriate? Should the articulation be *legato* or non-*legato*?

Let's close this fascinating and under-discussed subject with a look at the
opening of Debussy's celebrated Prelude *La Cathédrale engloutie*.

There are so many ways of approaching sound production in this piece's first
few bars, quite apart from the enormous controversy whereby at least half of
the pianistic population, including myself, plays bars 7–13 and related passages
at double the notated speed. You can draw the chords towards your body, as
though stroking a cat. You can do exactly the opposite too: imagine that you
are pushing the piano forwards – 'dip' into the keyboard on each chord and
create a wave-like movement from note to note. There is even a minority of

players who advocate organ-like finger substitutions so that the top line of the right hand is beautifully connected and overlapped throughout. And there is much more to consider here too – balancing, voicing, *rubato*, flexibility. Do we play the music in strict time, or do we try to make the lowest first notes of each phrase more significant, as though the chords that come above them are ripples or offshoots? 'Option one' teachers may well battle out these questions for themselves before insisting on a complete generic choice for everyone on earth, whilst 'option two' teachers would keep the questions coming in each lesson, time after time. 'Option three' teachers would be much more relaxed about all of the issues, casually trying each one out, ideally in a studio with two pianos, in which one could imagine a musical 'dialogue' in operation, with first one phrase being played by student, then answered by teacher and vice versa. Variation in touch, tempo, voicings, pedalling and orchestration would be thrown in the air, not with any questioning as such, but rather with an aura of quiet serenity as each approach is first presented, then respected and finally assimilated into the infinite pool of creative possibility.

Musical notation is only a limited framework from which receptive artistry can begin. To understand the parameters of possibilities that exist is to become fully conscious of an almost unlimited range of choice. It is the performer's duty and challenge to make his choices sound authoritative. When this is achieved, the overall performance will have integrity.

15 Beyond Ürtext

Curators

Since 1945 musicians have become increasingly historically aware, with many embracing period instruments and turning to musicologists for authenticity in terms of performance practice. In addition to the numerous Ürtext and authoritative performing editions that have accumulated over the decades, authors such as Thurston Dart and Howard Ferguson have had an enormous impact on the way many pianists approach works of the 18th century in particular. We have also become much more conscious in the past 70 years of the importance of reading around the keyboard literature. We should celebrate the ease with which information and opportunities can reach us in the 21st century, because knowledge is most certainly power! However, for practising pianists at all levels there are real dangers in enacting the role of musical 'curator'. We run the risk of having an overwhelming amount of data with which to work. For this reason, it is important for pianists to develop organisation techniques in order to sensitively select the source material from which they should work. In baroque repertoire, confidence and positive delivery are everything. Without these attributes, it will be very hard for performers to sound authoritative when it comes to realising ornamentation, dealing with hotly contested issues such as the use of notes *inégales* or double-dotting in pieces such as the D major Fugue from Book One of Bach's *Well-Tempered Clavier*. Of course, there are just as many 'conviction' issues in repertoire from the other centuries.

Musicians should never stop being curious and never lose the quest to re-evaluate interpretive decisions about works they may have performed successfully for decades, however if too much contradictory information is considered at a single time, if compromises are made simply to avoid offending any particular writer or adjudicator, then there is a strong likelihood of lacklustre music making. We should never lose sight of the fact that any one performance is just that – we all have the opportunity to replay and reconsider our decisions. So, it is much better to embrace strongly your interpretive decisions in one concert performance than to try to moderate your interpretive choices in a bid to please everyone. This will energise and lead to more confidence and conviction, even if a few of your listeners may be offended in the process!

Traditionalists

Alongside misguided students who try in vain to reproduce performances of their favourite pianists stand those who refuse to accept any interpretation unless it is in a particular 'school' or tradition. In the previous chapter, we referred to 'totalitarian' teachers who insist that it is only their way of playing Tchaikovsky that counts. Commonly, reasons given for such inflexibility are historical: for example, the dogmatic guru in question may claim a direct lineage to Tchaikovsky, simply because their teacher was a student of a student who studied the work directly with a student of the composer himself! Clearly this approach to pedagogy, whilst fascinating and historically intriguing, is negative and destructive, implying that only an elite and privileged group of musicians count for anything with regard to particular repertoire. It is also extremely limiting to the composer and his music; anyone who has worked with a composer knows how democratic and free most of them tend to be with their own music. As pianists, we can see this most easily perhaps in the works of Chopin, as there are several published versions of the same piece, showing clearly how flexible and pragmatic his musical imagination was: Chopin clearly did not believe in limiting his music to a fixed final version!

On the subject of Chopin, we have all heard anecdotes and met students who refuse to play his Mazurkas because they are not Polish, and therefore cannot cope with the folk-inspired rhythmic vibrancy of these miniature masterpieces.[54] I have even heard a wonderful artist admit that he refuses to play any Debussy or Ravel, simply because he does not speak the French language! Ultimately such a stance is negative and limiting, though it does imply modesty as well as an acknowledgement that language plays a seminal, often under-explored element in the musical make-up of our composers.[55] There is always something inspiring and convincing about performing Russian concertos with Russian orchestras, collaborating with English musicians in Vaughan Williams and Finzi, or working with Americans in Copland and Gershwin. The obvious caveat to all of this is political: we should always remember that nationality does not ensure musical authority. We risk racism and bigotry if we deny musicians the right to explore their own interpretations of certain works written by composers foreign to them in terms of geography. Music is a universal language that breaks down cultural barriers. There will never be one definitive way of approaching masterpieces, and the most sympathetic listeners, teachers, critics and performers all realise this.

Freedom within boundaries

In Chapter 15 of *Piano Technique in Practice*, fidelity to the text, aural photography and the infinite possibilities of interpretation within the fixed limits of instructions on the printed score were discussed.[56] Let's retrace textual fidelity

---

54   One only need listen to the exquisite recordings of the Chinese pianist Fou T'Song to realise how misguided this attitude truly is!
55   Many examples of how language influences musical phrasing could be given, but perhaps the most striking and immediate examples can be seen in the works of the Czech composer Leoš Janáček – look at his *12 Popular Moravian Dances* for examples of the way language can profoundly affect rhythm.
56   See pages 144–50 of *Piano Technique in Practice*. 'Aural photography' takes a considerable effort and energy. Though it is unquestionably a prerequisite of authoritative playing, it should be practised with caution. It is all too easy to lose sight of the bigger, emotionally charged picture when there are so many rules and regulations that need to be followed!

for some further consideration, given that it is important to find an artistically convincing means of balancing musical discipline with creativity and freedom.

We should never forget that performance is so much more than mere 'aural photography'. Within the parameters of superficially 'fixed' rules, there is an infinite range of contrasted possibilities for experimentation and consideration. This is an enormous subject, but for starters it is worth recalling that many conventional signs, terms and symbols may mean entirely different things from one composer in one historical period to the next.[57]

By its very nature, music notation is extremely vague and approximate. One only needs to think of the basic distinctions of dynamics to prove this – within the boundaries of *pianissimo, piano, mezzo piano, mezzo forte, forte* and *fortissimo* there are infinite shades of colour. The same is true in terms of articulation. There are many different types of *staccato* possible on a modern grand piano, and it is up to the pianist to decide just how short or how long an individual *staccato* marking should be played. This can be clearly seen in Debussy's Étude 10, *pour les sonorités opposées* which shows how much variation is possible even within the realms of aural photography.

The leaning accents in the third bar can be played with forward pianistic movements, or with upward movements, or even by lifting the notes towards the torso. All three approaches are valid and can be convincing. In terms of the *mezzo staccato* semiquavers that follow, the pianist must experiment with length and intensity of touch. Again, there is no 'right' and 'wrong' approach. Overall, these four bars provide all sorts of different solutions in terms of tonal balance and harmonic hierarchy. Pianists should never feel that one approach is definitive and, indeed, it is refreshing to return to music like this and 'revoice' it on each performance or practice session!

Let's return again to the famous opening of Rachmaninov's Second Piano Concerto, Op.18.

---

57 For a fascinating and inspirational discussion of this subject, see *The Secret Life of Musical Notation* by Roberto Poli (Amadeus Press, 2010).

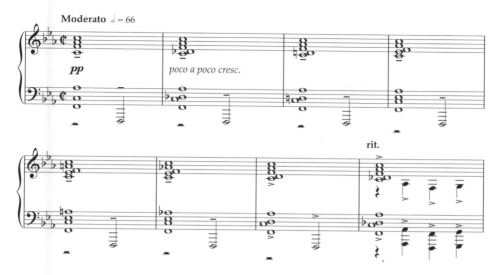

This is a fabulous test for the bass register of an instrument, and a glorious challenge for players in search of a dramatic and charismatic *crescendo* from the softest of chords through to the most thrilling of *fortissimos*. It is certainly both beneficial and interesting to prioritise different levels in the texture in turn, as you repeat this iconic phrase in practice. In particular, give more weight and depth of tone to the thumb notes in the right hand rather than to the highest notes. It is also exciting to try to play the whole phrase in one continuous pedal creating a wash of sound, yet always ensuring that definition is achieved through careful dynamics and balancing on each chord. Neither approach should be considered as 'better' than the other, though perhaps the latter would work more successfully in a large hall than a small teaching room.

In terms of dogmatism and 'doing the right thing', the opening of Rach 2 is controversial because of the evidence we have been left with; if one follows the directions on the published text, the pulse of ♩ = 66 is totally at odds with the composer's own famous and impressive recording (he starts slowly and gradually gets faster, making the second line of the concerto feel like a different tempo from bar 1). What to do? Clearly, both approaches can be justified. What would Rachmaninov have said?! It is important for all pianists who play this celebrated concerto to be completely familiar both with the text on the printed score as well as with Rachmaninov's interpretation. Ultimately, both approaches have their place and it is up to the individual interpreter to find integrity in any given performance. It will come from hard work, reflection and respect for the music; confidence, will develop and lead to real conviction and authority, whatever decisions are taken!

Technical reasons for textual rebellion

Pitfalls mainly occur in the practice of textual fidelity because the physical actions of playing the piano do not always correspond to aural realities, where written instructions relate to the aural result for the listener rather than to the physical approach for the pianist. Sadly, students frequently fail to understand this crucial difference. A musical score is not an instruction manual for a performer – it is a written 'transcription'; a work of art in which the composer will usually go as far as s/he can to show the integrity of their artistic vision. The physical practicalities of realising this vision will often mean that a composer's written instructions need to be blatantly ignored or challenged by performers. This phenomenon is perhaps most apparent in concertos: if a composer writes a prominent phrase for the solo pianist to play *piano* or *pianissimo* whilst the full orchestra are busy with thick-textured passagework, then the dynamic marking has to be reviewed if the audience wishes to hear the soloist at all!

This goes much further than merely rearranging dynamics. For many years, I greatly admired the beautiful richness of Jorge Bolet's *legatissimo* on record. I always took his approach to be one in which physical *legato* fingerwork was evident in every phrase. His richly overlapping *legato* technique sounds on record as though he is literally dovetailing passages from finger to finger as he plays scales with the deepest, richest tone imaginable. When I subsequently came across a film of Bolet playing Chopin's G minor Ballade, to my complete amazement I saw that much of his pianism did the complete opposite of what I imagined from his records: Bolet's fingers frequently lifted off the keys. Even though the sounds that came out of the piano were exquisitely rich and *legato*, the physical approach that produced them could perhaps be best described as 'non-*legato*'! For a while this unsettled me, until I realised that the only law-giver when it comes to music is the human ear – what sounds authoritative is what counts, and if the process of achieving aural authority is politically incorrect, then so be it!

Rebellion against the text can also be necessary from a rhythmic perspective. Defying motoric rhythms in practice can certainly help to overcome technical difficulties. The example below comes from one of the most challenging sections in Beethoven's A major Sonata, Op.101 (the development section of the finale, bars 209–12).

To take too literal an approach in terms of rhythmic exactitude and pulse when practising this section could lead to much physical tension, stiffness and anxiety. But all is not lost if you have the courage to 'bend' Beethoven's rhythms, at least in terms of your own private mental attitude and in the privacy of the practice studio! In this example, control will develop via selective delays on individual notes. Ultimately this is as much a mental as a literal phenomenon though, in practice, experience has shown that is really helpful to hold down the first semiquaver in each beat for longer than written. I also recommend holding down the fourth semiquaver of each beat in practice, then gradually shortening them with each repetition. Extending individual notes gives an increased feeling of spaciousness. As experience and confidence grow there will be no need to hold notes at all – the *tenutos* on the first or last semiquavers of each beat will become irrelevant, though it may still be useful to imagine that they are in place. They can evolve into simple 'mental tools', invisible delays of which no listener would ever be aware.

The excerpt below (bars 18–20 from Debussy's Second Étude) is marked *legato*, but is presented in the instrument's lower register.

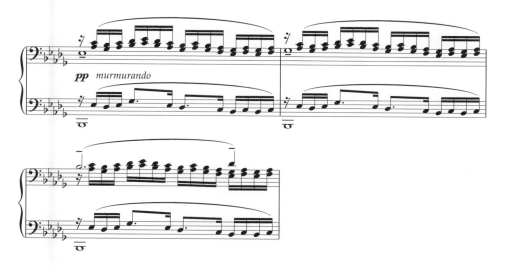

In order to achieve beautiful *legato* playing, this passage seems to demand a non-*legato*, *staccato leggiero* touch! To work with a literal physical overlap between each right-hand note is to risk a lack of clarity and control in a potentially muddy register. Here it is important to move away from literal instructions on the text – from the physical nature of playing. Working with a close *staccato* touch and pedal will make the audience feel that a *legato* sound world is being faithfully realised. Ironically, in examples like this one it is possible to get much more clarity and *legato* through light *staccato* fingerwork than through laborious dovetailing from semiquaver to semiquaver.

Finally, a few more treacherously demanding bars from Chopin's fast and furious B flat minor Prelude, Op.28 No.16, a piece we quoted from earlier (see page 29):

Here it is helpful to expand selected notes rhythmically and to adopt a *leggiero* non-*legato* touch. The music may appear charged and *legato*, but it will thrive and develop pianistically when rhythmic flexibility and detached finger-work are built up in the practice studio. The ferocious leaps and jumps in the left hand will remain uncomfortable and erratic if practised as written. In order to find confidence, it is helpful to lengthen the lower notes of each big intervallic leap, and to lighten the higher notes. Working with your eyes shut will also facilitate control. In terms of the right hand, the semiquavers become much easier when they are executed with a gentler touch. Do not try and be too conscientious here – overlapping *legato* work can restrict energy and movement, making the hand less pliable and flexible. This whole Prelude will benefit from work in small sections. Try to avoid 'sitting' on notes for longer than necessary – by developing subtle pedalling and a delicate *leggiero* touch the physical demands and angular melodic movements will become much easier to handle. The fact that the piece is so fast means that delivery will sound more *legato* than cumbersome literal playing that tries to bind each semiquaver together. Sometimes too much honesty can be a very bad thing indeed!

Final thoughts

At the most fulfilling level, music making is about communication and sharing. In a simplistic way, it can be seen as a two-way process: either between performer and listener, performer and teacher, or performer and composer. It is easy to see how this can be achieved, theoretically at least, by all pianists at every stage in the learning process. Chapter 4 concluded that real musical development is not consumer-driven. It is not about 'using' and moving on. And it is not about getting tired of old ideas! Indeed, it is very hard for anyone to separate the old from the new in piano playing; the musician is always a synthesis, a configuration of all past, present (and conceivably future) experiences, whether they appear positive, negative or neutral.

To avoid negative, stale and predictable approaches to piano playing in the long term it is important to share creativity with others. We should freely acknowledge influences as we ourselves influence others. This should be a universal phenomenon that transcends financial constraints. In art, there should be no secrets! Of course, there will always be pianists who 'pretend' to live publicly or consciously in denial of their past. Commonly this is seen when they airbrush the names of former teachers from their publicity material and conscious thoughts, even if privately or subconsciously they retain all that they have learnt from them! By denying influences but retaining the skills given to them from their former mentors, students may perhaps feel that they look more impressive. Is this 'musical vampirism'?! Certainly, it seems to be tied up with the totally misconceived notion that teaching the piano is to be avoided at all costs if you want to develop as a pianist. The glorious truth is the complete opposite: by giving – whether as a teacher, performer or conversationalist – you are receiving constantly. Teaching is one of the main ways in which all pianists can continue to learn and to grow throughout their lifespan not only as players, but also as artists and human beings.

Conversations on this subject with the Russian pianist and teacher Dina Parakhina (May 2016) proved both reassuring and inspirational. Dina believes that we pianists teach in order to keep music alive; we are not teaching in order to receive affection or gratitude! If you have truly succeeded in steeping your world with the inspirational fervour and glory of creativity via music, then a lack of polite acknowledgement, even a denial of influences from particular students to you personally, simply does not matter. Personally, I take great joy and comfort in telling others where my ideas come from. I love to constantly remember and thank my past mentors, both inwardly and outwardly. The public repetitive reiteration of gratitude feels exhilaratingly affirmative! It enables me to give even more to others each and every day as a musician and performer. It also seems to develop and realign the ideas of the past, making preconceived thoughts appear as new. It is simple to understand why this is the case: in piano playing, as in life itself, you receive more as you give more. By sharing and expressing gratitude, you energise and gain more in terms of confidence, control, ease and creativity as a pianist. In music, the art of teaching is the art of learning. For this reason, the financial aspect of piano pedagogy, whereby fees are paid by students to teachers, always sat uncomfortably with Franz Liszt and Ferruccio Busoni. Though they were in the fortunate position of not to needing tuition fees from the many students who came to study with them, there is something noble and beautiful about the fact that they always taught privately for nothing.

Music history is filled with students and colleagues who exploited others. Immediately I think of the Ken Russell film *Lisztomania* in which Wagner is cast as a vampire-like character who literally bites Liszt's neck and sucks blood out! Paul Meyers once wrote a fictional novel in which an ex-Nazi conductor gave all he could to a younger German conductor, who then took all of his technique and ideas on board before airbrushing him completely off the face of the earth, ensuring that his former mentor never conducted anywhere ever again.[58] And Busoni has not been given nearly enough credit for discovering and inspiring all kinds of ideas that others took up and for which they were given the credit. (I am thinking specifically here of Stravinsky, Schoenberg, Hindemith and others.[59])

But would Busoni have minded? Did Liszt resent the fact that Wagner evidently 'stole' his ideas and exploited them without proper acknowledgement? When an artist is truly buzzing with creativity, on fire with a need to communicate and share, such egotistical concerns mean very little. Passionate art protects against personal slight! Part one of this book mentioned that the prime human motivation for true pianist performers is a powerful need to share their love of music with others. This need is vital for all who truly love performing, composing, teaching or writing about music.

When music becomes your guiding force and inspiration, you have the strength to transcend human weaknesses and selfishness. Through faith in art you gain the power and wherewithal to transform the world you are a part of into a more beautiful place. That is the true, positive and exciting possibility that comes from the infinite power of music.

58   Paul Myers, *Concerto*, Century London, 1993.
59   See Erinn E. Knyt: *Ferruccio Busoni and His Legacy*, Indiana University Press, 2017.

Reviews of *The Foundations of Technique*

'Essential reading for any pianist.'
Amazon Reviewer

'Every pianist can benefit from this splendid book. Stuffed with sensible advice, it's the sum, one feels, of its author's long experience in playing, teaching and nurturing talent to the very highest level – handed to us all, effectively, on a plate. McLachlan looks at piano technique from every possible angle, from the hand's anatomy to how to manage awkward leaps and how to use the piano's pedals to finest effect. His writing is accessible, clear and authoritative; the book's layout is user-friendly and the suggested exercises more than valuable. As with the companion volume by McLachlan, *Piano Technique in Practice*, I can see how much I would have benefitted from this book had I had it when I was a student. But it's never too late: I fully intend to use its wealth and wisdom for my practising today.'
Amazon Reviewer

Review of *Piano Technique in Practice*

'An essential guide for teachers and students alike. Rather than dealing with technique as a separate entity, McLachlan takes us on a compelling musical journey, demonstrating how manual dexterity and such essential skills as developing musical memory evolve naturally out of a pianist's desire to fulfil their interpretative vision. I only wish I'd had this volume to hand when I was a student many moons ago!'
Amazon Reviewer